What readers say about Neil Humphreys' writing

"Anybody wanting to know more about Singapore, and especially Singaporeans, should skip all those boring guidebooks and read Neil Humphreys' books instead. They're humorous, entertaining and make you question whether he's even in the right country in the first place. Be prepared for stares all around while you're busy laughing your head off reading."
— **Amal Husnah Jamaludin**

"There's a reason to like Neil Humphreys' books. They're funny. I follow his books and learn stuff about my own country. I spend time laughing about his journeys until I get a tummy cramp."
— **Darren Ong**

"You can tell by the 'well-read' condition (ok…battered) copies of Neil Humphreys' books in local libraries just what Singaporeans think of his work. They aren't battered through disgust at this *ang moh* writing about their country; rather Neil's work is embraced for his unbridled enthusiasm and respect for their country. Neil deliberately jumped into local life with gusto and this has given him a unique perspective and understanding on Singapore culture. Neil Humphreys is to Singapore what Clive James is to London – an outsider that became an insider."
— **Kelly Jackson Nash**

"Neil's writing style is blatantly direct and strikingly witty. Be warned that you will be thrown off guard by his honesty and wittiness in every single page. I especially like his work in *Return to a Sexy Island*. He seems to know the changes in Singapore much better than the locals."
— **Richard Ng**

"Neil's a very naughty boy. He likes to play with himself in Singapore for our amusement. Neil has a wicked sense of humour, which makes his books irresistible."
— **Juliet McCully**

"At his humorous best, Neil Humphreys sizes up everything right and wrong about Singapore in his own unique way."
— **Keegan Gan**

"Neil's wit and humour never fails to brighten up my day. I was pleasantly surprised when he displayed another facet of his outstanding mastery for words when I read *Marina Bay Sins*. The suspense and drama contained within made me finish the book in double quick time!"
— **Roland Chua**

"Neil's done it again and again with his books. He gets Singapore in all its absurd contradictions but ultimately sees it for what it is – a wondrous work-in-progress. Takes one to know one I suppose."
— **Justin Deimen**

"As an *ang moh* who has completely assimilated into Singapore's social fabric, Neil's books, with their crisp and concise writing coupled with a generous peppering of Singlish and local slang, are a total delight to read. Just wish we could have more of his books!"
— **Amit Nagpal**

"What's not to love about our favourite foreign talent. Neil's books speak to us Singaporeans on so many levels and at all ages. He tickles our funny bones with his wit. Even if you're somewhat lacking in the humour department, there is bound to be something to make you laugh, unless you're a block of wood. Cheers to our beloved Singaporean-*ang moh*! Keep writing mate. There are bones to be tickled (and bills to be paid...)"
— **Sadie-Jane Nunis**

"My fave local *ang moh* author who offers an insightful, no-holds barred view on life in Singapore, give the man a Tiger and make him a Singaporean already!"
—**Yvonne Janet Schelkis-Sweeney**

Saving a Sexier Island

Notes from an Old Singapore

NEIL HUMPHREYS

Marshall Cavendish
Editions

© 2015 Marshall Cavendish International (Asia) Private Limited

Cover photo by Alvin Loh

Published by Marshall Cavendish Editions
An imprint of Marshall Cavendish International
1 New Industrial Road, Singapore 536196

Other Marshall Cavendish Offices
Marshall Cavendish Corporation. 99 White Plains Road, Tarrytown NY 10591-9001, USA • Marshall Cavendish International (Thailand) Co Ltd. 253 Asoke, 12th Flr, Sukhumvit 21 Road, Klongtoey Nua, Wattana, Bangkok 10110, Thailand • Marshall Cavendish (Malaysia) Sdn Bhd, Times Subang, Lot 46, Subang Hi-Tech Industrial Park, Batu Tiga, 40000 Shah Alam, Selangor Darul Ehsan, Malaysia

Marshall Cavendish is a trademark of Times Publishing Limited

National Library Board, Singapore Cataloguing-in-Publication Data
Humphreys, Neil.
Saving a sexier island : notes from an old Singapore / Neil Humphreys. – Singapore: Marshall Cavendish Editions, [2015]
pages cm
ISBN: 978-981-4634-09-0 (paperback)
1. Humphreys, Neil – Travel – Singapore. 2. Singapore – Description and travel. 2. Singapore – Social life and customs. I. Title.

DS609.7
915.9570453 — dc23   OCN905880470

Printed in Singapore by Markono Print Media Pte Ltd

Acknowledgements

THESE JOURNEYS usually begin with me informing my wife and daughter that I'll be on the road for six months. To help me cope with the ordeal, my wife hid her grief really, really well. I must thank her for that.

Marshall Cavendish, Pansing and all the bookstores that have supported my titles ever since I used to sneak in on weekends and move my books to their most prominent shelves deserve my eternal gratitude. I don't do that any more of course. I sneak in on Tuesday nights instead.

But this book, perhaps more than any other, has been inspired by Singaporeans, nurtured by Singaporeans and completed by Singaporeans. The bloggers, the civic activists, the petitioners, the community groups and heritage sites, the nature trekkers and the conservationists, the history lovers and the eco-warriors all motivated me to search for the island's older, sexier bits.

This tour would also not have been possible without the tireless work of the National Heritage Board, the National Library Board, the National Archives of Singapore, NParks and the Public Utilities Board. The Hantu Bloggers, the Singapore Canoe Federation and ACRES, too, displayed an eagerness to help that was humbling. I'm just glad I didn't break, drop or drown anything.

These journeys usually end with me informing my wife and daughter that I'll be home for a while. To help me resettle, my wife hid her joy really, really well.

But my daughter is mostly pleased to get her fellow explorer back. So this book is dedicated to her. Thanks for listening to all my adventure stories, mate.

But you've got to stop telling people that "Daddy's job is looking for sexy bits".

Prologue

SEBASTIAN VETTEL was staring at me. I wanted to punch him. I'm not a tough guy. He was a waxwork figure. The odds were marginally in my favour.

But my rage was real. I hadn't anticipated bumping into the Formula 1 driver at Sentosa's Imbiah Lookout. The summit of Singapore's premier tourist destination was never previously known for its international celebrities. It was known for its cable car station, that weird, whirly thing that offers panoramic views of the Indonesian haze and Man with the Snake. I had first visited Sentosa in late 1996 and Man with the Snake was usually found at the Imbiah Lookout. He was often the first person to greet new Sentosa arrivals, fresh off the cable car. His greeting always felt slightly incongruous. Welcome to Sentosa. What do you think of my snake? Isn't it big? But I found his presence strangely comforting, a quintessentially Singaporean experience. If Man with the Snake was wandering about the place, all was right with Sentosa. But he was gone and I was stuck with Sebastian Vettel.

This wasn't Sentosa. But it did feel a lot like New Singapore.

And then I saw that Images of Singapore was closed. That was the point of my family's visit to the Imbiah Lookout, to visit the quaint attraction that depicted the country's backstory. My daughter had recently discovered history and wanted to learn about "old people". There were no short-term plans to visit my mother-in-law, so I settled on Images of Singapore instead. The exhibition might have been a little worn around the edges perhaps, but I remembered the place fondly, a benign look at the country's history and cultural diversity with a heavy-handed banging of the nationalistic drum every now and then. Images of Singapore was one of the few obvious tourist attractions left that was entirely devoted to the cultural fabric of the country itself. And it had been shunted out of the way. Madame Tussauds was taking its place. Stamford Raffles had given way to Lady Gaga.

"This is bloody outrageous," I ranted to my wife, my daughter and the smug Sebastian Vettel staring back at me through the window. "Why has Images of Singapore been replaced by Madame Tussauds? Why doesn't this country respect its own heritage? Why didn't Madame Tussauds make a waxwork of me?"

"Calm down, Neil," my wife interjected. "It's 8pm, I'm hungry and your daughter needs to pee."

This wasn't quite what I had in mind when I returned to Singapore in 2011. I've got nothing against Madame Tussauds. My childhood fascination with history was fuelled by a school trip to London's waxwork exhibition, where I was introduced to Henry VIII's six wives, learned about Guy Fawkes' plot to blow up the Houses of Parliament and narrowly avoided soiling my underwear when my best mate Ross jumped out from behind Jack the Ripper. But a local attraction being consumed by a larger, foreign entity was another sign of these so-called sexy times. I called the Sentosa customer service line and a staff member explained that Madame Tussauds had taken over the glorious colonial property at Imbiah Lookout (a military hospital in the

19th Century and a historic location in itself), relegating Images of Singapore to a supplementary attraction, an optional add-on. And his caveat was a real kick in the teeth. Standalone tickets for Images of Singapore were no longer available. They were bundled together with admission to Madame Tussauds. On the Sentosa website, Images of Singapore was trumpeted as "a journey to the very soul of the nation". And to get to the very soul of this nation, you must buy a ticket to a foreign tourist attraction first.

Like many others, I initially succumbed to New Singapore's charms. I was lured home from Australia by the sudden sex appeal. My former lover welcomed me back with open arms and I was grateful to be back in her sweaty bosom. And what a bosom it was. She had all the right figures (heading towards 6.9 million at one point). From the Woodlands Waterfront to Marina Bay, she'd undergone a dramatic makeover from top to bottom, complete with long, slender glassy curves and regular Botox injections of fresh billionaires. She was cleaner, but trashier; greener, but grubbier; sexier, but sleazier. Suddenly, she was up all night long and eager to please. She was a party animal. I was smitten and followed her everywhere, exploring her delectable Southern Ridges (magical), her humorous side (Universal Studios), her hardheadedness (Marina Bay Sands) and her flawless spine (the Railway Corridor, where I was detained for trespassing).

Superficially, Singapore had everything. She was glamorous, desirable, expensive, sparkly and omnipresent. But then so are the Kardashians. They are also unattainable, beyond the reach of the masses, painfully transparent and a little hollow. It's only a matter of time before they are invited to appear at the Singapore Grand Prix. But the more I explored New Singapore, the more I struggled with a nagging question. Who is she for? She looks terrific in a cocktail dress, but who is this sexy island really flirting with? The international elite flocks to the country for the annual grand prix, but Singaporeans suffer the road closures and traffic jams. Overseas investors have flooded the island to buy into the "Monte Carlo of Asia" dream, also known as "the Monaco of Asia", "the Switzerland of Asia" or the "*kelong* capital of Asia", depending on whom you speak to. But property prices have soared beyond the means of some Singaporean families. Between the publication of my book *Return to a Sexy Island* and the production of the subsequent TV series a year later, my perception changed. The tide of public opinion had pulled me in a different direction. Singaporeans were teaching me what was truly sexy about our home.

But the TV series was the real turning point. Initially, I learned that I was too tall for TV, too lanky for the wardrobe, too sweaty for the camera, too dark around the eyes to be an artiste and cursed with too scruffy a hairstyle to be a professional host (as the episodes progressed, I fully expected to be replaced by a pale, dry-skinned, bald, muscular dwarf). But I also discovered the contradiction, the growing hypocrisy. Casinos and Sentosa Cove penthouses are sexy in an obvious, clichéd sense, but they are increasingly losing their attraction. There are only so many times one can wander past wealthy foreigners carrying shopping bags through the ghastly Shoppes mall at Marina Bay Sands before the novelty wears thin. After filming at the swankiest, tackiest nightclubs and bars that had mushroomed across Marina Bay to serve the international trust fund babies, I suggested the island's most glamorous nightspot was a hawker centre. When I examined the country's burgeoning arts and theatre scene, I opted to end the episode at a delightful dance club in a quiet community centre. After feigning interest in the fleets of Ferraris and Lamborghinis that come out to play along Orchard Road on the weekends, I championed the humble bicycle and its cycling paths and park connectors. Eventually, inevitably, the memos reached me. What's so sexy about this stuff? Hawker centres, community centres and pushbikes do not pander to the privileged. They don't fit the sexy narrative of New Singapore. We're hip. We're groovy. We're happening. We're moving forward. Traditional, local Singapore is old hat. We all live in an international playground, reaping the financial rewards of those crazy rich Asians. Old Singapore is as dead as the residents of Bukit Brown Cemetery. Singaporeans are tomorrow people. No one cares about yesterday.

Only they do. They really do. And they've come forward, in their tens of thousands, at Bukit Brown Cemetery, at Speakers Corner, at public symposiums and meet-the-people sessions, to speak up for Bukit Brown, Rochor Centre, Chek Jawa, old HDB flats and communities; anything and everything that has kept the fraying umbilical cord between Singapore and the Singaporean in place. They're searching for something more substantial than a pay cheque, something identifiable, something comforting. Hotel complexes, artificial gardens and gentrified districts have their commercial appeal, but no emotional connection. As the foreigners swarm through the arrivals hall at Changi Airport and the endless urban tinkering continues, locals have been left lost; strangers in their own land. With every National Day Parade, more questions pile up. What *is* Singaporean? What are we defined by? What is unique to our island? What can we identify with? Is it a family-run laksa stall in Katong or a casino complex owned by a billionaire hotel magnate from Las Vegas? What makes me Singaporean? Do I know all the words to *Majulah Singapura*? Do I eat rojak? Do I play *sepak takraw* at the community club? Could I do all three at once during a flag-waving ceremony?

The questions were getting harder to answer. Singaporeans were living in a land of confusion. The economic Blitzkrieg was exhausting and disorienting, so they stole a peek over their shoulder. They liked what they saw. We're all suckers for sentimentality.

Nostalgia took hold. From Bukit Brown bloggers to amateur photographers recording condemned buildings and civic activists calling for housing estates to be protected, heritage became hip. Old school became cool. And I was delighted. For years, I thought I was the only one. In my previous Singapore books, I had devoted entire chapters to the need to save, restore and preserve, but then I'm addicted to nostalgia and hoarding keepsakes that evoke memories of "the good old days".

I believe anything of personal historical value must be kept. When my daughter inadvertently swallowed her first tooth, I sifted through her waste for two days. Using rubber gloves and disposable chopsticks, I searched in vain for that tiny speck of white enamel as the tears flowed and the stench melted my face. When my wife questioned my actions, I cried: "Because it is my daughter's first tooth! Because she cannot have another in her life." It was like that powerful scene in *The Crucible*, if you can picture John Proctor bent over a toilet bowl, elbow-deep in his daughter's shit.

I never did find the tooth.

But I am determined to find a sexier island. That's a lame segue, I know, but there's nothing lame about the glorious, inspirational Singaporeans who are writing, blogging, chasing and capturing that elusive, personal connection with their country while it still exists. While the New Singapore of Sentosa Cove rapidly turns into a ghost town (stop laughing), the Old Singapore of Jalan Besar and Tiong Bahru is finding its art deco curves being wolf-whistled at. As tourists visit Madame Tussauds to take selfies with international celebrities, more Singaporeans are heading into historic nooks and crannies to find authentic images of Singapore.

And as I stared into the eyes of Sebastian Vettel, I decided to do the same. New Singapore was done and dusted. As the country prepared to celebrate its 50th birthday, I wanted to explore what was left of Singapore's old soul.

Old Singapore
Neil's Top 50 Places

Not to Scale

Old Singapore: Neil's Top 50 places

1. Dragon Playground
2. Toa Payoh's Observation Tower
3. Balestier Plain
4. Sweetlands Bakery
5. Mustafa Centre
6. Rochor Centre
7. Thieves Market
8. Jalan Besar
9. Kam Leng Hotel
10. Emerald Hill
11. No. 38 Oxley Road
12. National Museum of Singapore
13. St John's Island
14. Lazarus Island
15. Baba House
16. Blair Plain
17. Kampong Silat
18. Tiong Bahru
19. Historic air-raid shelter
20. Fort Siloso
21. Alexandra Hospital
22. Queenstown Stadium
23. Singapore's first HDB flats
24. Queenstown Library
25. Pulau Hantu Kecil
26. Pulau Hantu Besar
27. Haw Par Villa
28. Colbar Café
29. Beauty World
30. Memories at Old Ford Factory
31. Little Guilin Park
32. Bukit Batok Nature Park
33. Jurong Bird Park
34. Old Choa Chu Kang Road bus stops
35. Neo Tiew Estate
36. ACRES Wildlife Rescue Centre
37. Sungei Buloh Wetland Reserve
38. Kranji War Cemetery
39. Upper Seletar "Rocket" Tower
40. Last *kampong kopitiam* in Singapore
41. Matilda House
42. Coney Island
43. Johore Battery
44. Old Changi Hospital
45. Joo Chiat
46. Siglap's last HDB flats
47. Old Kallang Airport
48. Dakota Crescent
49. Haji Lane
50. Singapore's rivers

One

THE UNCLE JOINED ME at the food court table. He was extraordinarily skinny with long bony fingers. His body was lost behind a grubby, loose-fitting vest. He smiled at me. He had more long, straggly hairs on his chin than he had teeth.

"Where you from ah?" he asked, cutting to the chase.

"I'm from here," I mumbled, not particularly keen on going through every stamp in the passport.

"Cannot be, right? You don't look Singaporean."

This snap judgment is not an uncommon one. Depending on my mood, I might occasionally ask for a broad description of what the average Singaporean looks like, just in case I spot one at the National Day Parade or stumble across another fleeing from the Whitley Road Detention Centre, something like that. How does one look more Singaporean? Should my skin be lighter or darker? Should I dress head to toe in white? Should I grow out the ginger in my beard and pass myself off as the late Ah Meng's offspring?

"No, I wasn't born in Singapore," I admitted. "But I've lived in Singapore, on and off, since 1996."

"Wah, 1996, you're practically Singaporean."

"You just said I wasn't."

"No lah, just kidding. But a long time, eh? You married, got kids?"

"Yah, I've got one daughter."

He shook his head wearily and peered down at the leftovers on my plate. Then he waggled a bony finger at me. "Not enough," he muttered. "You must know Singapore already. Have one for you, have one for Lee Kuan Yew."

"Hasn't he got three children already?"

The uncle laughed, far too loudly. It wasn't that funny. Families at other tables stared at the lanky *ang moh* and the old man seated across from each other at the dinner table. It was hardly *When Harry Met Sally*. He eyed my leftovers again. And then he insulted me.

"So what do you do ah?"

"I'm, er, a writer," I stuttered. "I'm just starting a new book now, actually."

The uncle's eyes widened.

"Ah, you're like me," he said. "Unemployed."

Those were his exact words. He had offended my profession. He had ridiculed my livelihood. He had insulted the written word itself and, according to my wife later, he had a point.

Struggling to speak as the bruises swelled across my wounded soul, I sputtered: "No, I'm not unemployed. I'm a writer, really. That's why I'm here now. I'm exploring Old Singapore, your Singapore, before it disappears. So I'm starting here, where it started for me when I first arrived on the island all those years ago. This town's history is also my history. I'm going to find all the old places, the traditional things that people like you remember; the things that really are Singaporean, the places that should matter to people. And I'm going to put them all in a book with photos and everything."

"Yah, I understand… Definitely cannot make much money right?"

He gestured towards my empty plate.

"Can buy me *makan* or not?"

I gave him $5. He said that was too much money. I told him not to worry. He thanked me and hoped my tour of Old Singapore was a success. I wished him well. He pocketed the change.

I could only be in Toa Payoh.

When I first moved to Singapore, I lived in Toa Payoh and passed the town's Dragon Playground every day. It's impossible to forget the first time our eyes met across Lorong 6. I thought someone had slipped LSD into my Kickapoo. At a bend in the road, the tiled behemoth suddenly appeared from nowhere in the most incongruous of settings, as if it had been evicted from Tolkien's Middle Earth and dumped in a housing estate sand pit. I had to be hallucinating. On first inspection, the Toa Payoh Dragon Playground seemed to be the only masochistic playground in the world designed to hurt children.

As time passed, the old dragon grew on me. The quirky structure was a comforting fixed point in an ever-evolving Toa Payoh. It anchored the old town and offered an imposing welcome to cars trundling in off the expressway. Mostly, I liked the playground because it was offbeat and colourfully irreverent; unusual qualities in the 1970s, let alone in the sanitised, controlled environment of New Singapore. Strolling along Lorong 6 now, I passed one of those new, plastic, eco-friendly, space-age children's playgrounds, full of sloping beams and whirly metallic structures that suggest the architect had been watching *Interstellar* and smoking marijuana when he drew up the plans. Modern playgrounds are Kubrickian. They're also a bit crap.

I reached the bend of Lorong 6, climbed the small concrete staircase and met the dragon. The housing blocks that once bordered the playground had gone, replaced by patches of grass. The green plain had an eerie feel, like a poppy field on an old World War I battleground. I was aware that the blocks had been earmarked for the en-bloc redevelopment programme, but I was still surprised that they had vanished so quickly – hundreds of family homes erased with characteristic haste and efficiency. Sentimentality is not a social value commonly associated with New Singapore.

But the imperious Dragon Playground lived on, standing alone in the dusky field, the last survivor of its razed kingdom. In 1979, HDB, to its eternal credit, commissioned its gifted, in-house designer Khor Ean Ghee to come up with something Singaporean. He created a dragon, with a head made of orange terrazzo tiles and a wavy spine of steel-ribbed rails that provided a pathway to the head, where a pair of slides jutted out from each side. A couple of tyre swings were added and the Dragon sat on a sandpit. In 1979, Singaporeans had never seen anything like it. To be honest, the rest of the world still hasn't seen anything like it. Its appeal lies in its daftness. In 2012, Toa Payoh's dragon was selected as one of the world's top 15 playgrounds in a New York blog. Before the bulldozers moved in, the protests began (no one staged a sit-in at the sandpit and waved placards at passing policemen. Some stern letters were sent to the newspapers and a couple of terrific blog posts were written. In Singapore, that was more than enough). The dragon earned a reprieve, for a while at least. It's a hazardous business to label anything irreplaceable.

Only three elements of the demolished housing estate remained. There was the concrete path leading to the old playground, the Dragon itself and a rusting sign providing visitors with a list of dos and don'ts. The most obvious "don't" that I immediately ignored was the stipulation that the playground was for the under-12s only. With childish glee, I jumped onto the dragon's spine via its rear entrance and pondered the mythical beast's anatomy. Biologically speaking, had I entered through the dragon's sphincter? With impeccable timing, I had become something of an expert on the subject. My daughter had recently dragged me to the superb human body exhibition at the Singapore Science Centre, where children were given the ingenious opportunity of moving through an extraordinary playground that was shaped like the human body. We climbed through a mouth, went down an oesophagus slide, waded through brown, foamy blocks in the digestive system and so on. As an anatomically appropriate finale, we finished the exhibition by squeezing through a narrow gap in a stretched, rubbery wall. It must be the only educational exhibit where you leave literally looking like shit. When my daughter returned to school, she delighted in showing off her expanded vocabulary by telling her teacher how "Daddy helped to push me through a really big sphincter".

So I made my way through the Dragon's bottom and along its spine, stopping at its tallest point. The old girl was in remarkably good condition. The reds, blues and yellows of her ribs had retained their vibrancy and the head didn't appear to be missing tiles. I was also rather high off the ground, almost a couple of metres up, with only a small, steel ribcage for protection. That's not a criticism, quite the opposite. The playground's design was edgy and offered a degree of risk-taking seldom provided for younger, strawberry generations. The Dragon was a reminder of a more independent time and place for children, not just for Singaporeans, but for me too. As I stood at the top of the ribcage, I found myself returning to my childhood. Growing up on an East London housing estate, we also had children's playgrounds, which were quaint places filled with small slides and swings for toddlers. But we had adventure playgrounds as well, where the older kids went to die.

Looking back, I now believe that the town council's resources were lavished on the toddler playgrounds, while the leftover bricks, timber planks, shards of glass and rusty, tetanus-infected nails were thrown onto a weed-filled dump and left to Igor, the hammer-happy apprentice, to bang something together for the older kids. In my hometown of Dagenham, the deadly centrepiece of our adventure playground was a rotten wooden platform known as "the jump". It was at least two storeys high. If memory serves, the platform was supposed to have ropes attached to make the descent safer, but Igor never got around to that particular job because he was too busy eating clumps of mud in the corner. So it became "the jump", where the ape boys flung themselves off the top to impress young girls. The ape boys were the kids in my class who were prodigiously well-developed, not just for boys, but for diplodocuses. They always made fun of my reluctance to jump. On one occasion, dark forces colluded to push me off the edge. As the ape boys mocked my cowardice, my best friend Ross pointed out that a girl I had a heart-stabbing crush on was looking up at me from below.

"Is she still looking? She's still looking, right," I muttered nervously to Ross. "Right, that's it. I'm doing 'the jump'. You ready? I'm ready. She's still looking? OK, this is it. I'm jumping. Three, two, one… Argh, I've broke me fucking leg."

That girl never did go out with me.

My point is, older children's playgrounds were tinged with a degree of risk and an implicit trust that kids would mostly do the right thing. Neither the children nor the playgrounds were buffeted by cotton wool. The Dragon Playground certainly wasn't. At the top of her head, I contemplated going down the slide. I can't lie. I was apprehensive. The slide was made of stone. Now, there's risk taking. And then there's dry-roasted testicles. But I noticed passers-by watching me in Lorong 6, like the elusive girl from my childhood imploring me to leap from "the jump". I squeezed my adult frame between the sides and forced myself slowly, agonisingly, down a children's slide made of stone. The friction was vicious. When I passed the bend at the end, I emitted a slight squeak of repressed pain. I got up and checked for holes in the back of my shorts. I expected to be greeted by the bloody remains of a baboon's pink bottom.

But I survived. And so has Toa Payoh's Dragon Playground.

It started to drizzle so I took shelter beneath the dragon's head and wondered how many Singaporeans had done likewise since 1979. For generations, the indigenous creature had provided an escape for young and old to temporarily get away from claustrophobic living conditions, the heat of the kitchen, argumentative neighbours, screaming siblings, *kiasu* parents, too much homework and maybe, occasionally, not enough love. Friendships were forged, games were invented, imaginations were fired, girlfriends were kissed and maybe one or two babies were conceived. I'm certain there must be a few "dragon babies" in Toa Payoh, but they weren't made on that slide.

The friction burns don't bear thinking about.

SPLASHING THROUGH PUDDLES, I skipped along Toa Payoh Lorong 6 towards the jolly green penis. In an earlier book, I mocked the Toa Payoh tower that stands proudly in the town park. I might have suggested that the slender edifice, in a certain light, could be passed off as a male organ riddled with gangrene. Older and wiser now, I peered through the persistent rain to marvel at Toa Payoh's architectural gem. It still looked like a bulbous green penis in need of medical attention.

And that's a good thing. Ignoring the phallic symbolism for a moment – which is rather difficult – try and consider the unique cultural value of this magnificent monument to the more brutal aspects of 1970s architecture. There really is nothing else quite like it in Singapore, or anywhere else for that matter. Whether that's cause for consternation or celebration depends on one's point of view. But I'm strangely drawn to imposing, monolithic structures. It's not so much a hankering for the town planning ideals of a totalitarian regime as it is a childhood obsession with that indelible image of the Statue of Liberty sticking out of the beach at the end of *Planet of the Apes*. Otherworldly buildings excite me.

In the north of England, there is a remarkable sculpture called the Angel of the North. Built on a grassy hill that was once a slagheap, the iron structure with outstretched arms like radiators is a stunning tribute to Newcastle's coal-mining past and industrial heritage; a colossal, intimidating piece of work that can be seen from miles around. Thanks to its size and lofty positioning, the sculpture boasts one of those bizarre statistics often trumpeted by tourism boards. A different person sees the Angel of the North every second. I vividly remember reading that tidbit on the information panel and my wife being unconvinced.

"Well, that's a load of rubbish," she sniffed. "There's hardly anyone here."

She pointed at the deserted fields that surrounded the sculpture and the mostly empty car park. "See, there are only about 10 people."

"You think one person visits every second?" I wondered.

"That's what they've written here. Idiots."

"They don't mean actual visitors. That would be 600 different people every 10 minutes. They'd be queuing for miles.

They mean people who see it from cars, lorries and buses. People who see it from the road."

"Oh, do they? Well, they should make it clearer then. It's a bloody eyesore anyway."

Some might say the same about the Toa Payoh tower. Like the Angel of the North, it's certainly an unusual sight (and site) and an acquired taste. But it is steeped in history and – I was surprised to learn from the excellent Toa Payoh Heritage Trail information panel – older than I thought. The Observation Tower was built in 1972 (the capital letters come from the National Heritage Board, suggesting that Observation Tower is the building's proper name and making it a contender for the most literal moniker in Singapore). Two years older than me, the Observation Tower provided the backdrop for many a wedding album through the '70s and '80s. Countless Toa Payoh couples – and others from elsewhere, since Toa Payoh was the island's first complete satellite town – posed among the park's Weeping Willows for their wedding photographs.

Students once tolerated the natural environment and prepared for upcoming exams in the park. Courting couples had picnics and locals worked on their tai chi at dawn, all within the shadow of the 25m-high tower. Anyone who has lived in Toa Payoh has a memory of the place. Personal memories greeted me in every direction. My first weekend in Singapore was spent feeding *ikan bilis* (dried anchovies) to the turtles in its pond. My future wife and I also had picnics beneath the stone pagodas to stretch our meagre resources. The three trees planted in a triangular formation to the immediate left of the tower belong to my family (we bought and planted them by contributing to NParks' wonderful adopt-a-tree programme shortly after my daughter was born. She still has the certificate on her bedroom wall). And, while doing research for a previous book, I fell off my bike beside the tower in a foolhardy attempt to pedal through a monsoonal storm.

Old Singapore surrounds the Observation Tower, but that doesn't mean you can touch it. I stepped across a small tiled path that covered the little landscaped moat and discovered that the entrance was locked. The Urban Redevelopment Authority (URA) gave the tower conservation status in 2009 and my ego assumes I played a small part in that. After I published my observations of the green penis in 2006, I received emails and letters from intrepid explorers who had sought out the Toa Payoh monument (and most agreed with my phallic imagery, I'm proud to say). At subsequent book signings, the green penis invariably worked its way into the conversation at some point. I have found myself discussing Toa Payoh's Observation Tower with readers more often than, say, Marina Bay Sands. That's as it should be. So I was thoroughly delighted when the URA heeded my advice and wrapped the tower in heritage-protected bubble wrap.

It's just unfortunate that the bubble wrap is stuck on with so much red tape.

The place was less welcoming than ever before, with a gate grille and a padlock borrowed from Alcatraz. The tower has been saved from both the bulldozers and its own people. It's a slightly paternalistic, patronising trend to preserve a heritage site, only to hide it behind a padlock. Can residents be trusted enough to respect their own history? If not, then the odd nod towards Old Singapore smacks of tokenism. The museumification of Toa Payoh's Observation Tower is likely to be replicated elsewhere. Save it. Repair it. Paint it. Hide it. The Angel of the North, like the Dragon Playground, can be touched, felt and experienced. The Observation Tower feels like a museum exhibit under lock and key. Look, but don't touch.

But it's still there. The mad phallic symbol lives on. As the drizzle gave way to a downpour, I dashed for cover at a sheltered bench outside the public toilets. A middle-aged guy sat at the other end. He unfolded a newspaper, fashioned a rectangular pillow of sorts, rolled onto his side and went to sleep. I stretched out and joined him, watching the hypnotic raindrops fall on Toa Payoh's most famous erection.

Now it's been gazetted, Toa Payoh's Dragon Playground will be removing the skin off small children for years to come.

Toa Payoh's Observation Tower remains one of the finest erections in Singapore.

Two

I BLUSH when I think of Balestier. When I first arrived and settled in the neighbouring town of Toa Payoh, the warnings came thick and fast. Don't go Balestier after dark, ah. Balestier not safe one. Balestier very dirty. Balestier not like Toa Payoh, Balestier very old already. Balestier got many problems; too many KTV lounges; too many *ah peks*; too many *ah bengs*; too many hookers: *ang moh* like you cannot make it.

I was mugged twice in London, an old school friend was arrested for drug dealing and another was killed in a nightclub fight. My family's East End history skirted the fringes of petty crime and I'm not entirely sure if any of the clothes in my childhood wardrobe were legally acquired. I thought I might cope with a flirty *xiao mei mei* shouting "hi, ham-sum" across a *bak kut teh* stall.

But I bowed to the local knowledge of my new Singaporean friends. Balestier mostly remained off my beaten track. I'm rather embarrassed to note that my five previous books on Singapore scarcely mention that community steeped in rich heritage with history oozing from almost every distinctive shophouse. And yet, interestingly, Balestier features prominently in my two Singapore novels, arguably for the same reasons I was advised to stay away:

its vibrant, sordid nightlife, colourful characters and ramshackle architecture. A compact, scruffy area that also houses HDB flats, condos and shophouses, Balestier isn't like anywhere else in Singapore.

Plus a KTV hostess once accosted me there. Together with the establishment's doorman, she was quite insistent that I pop inside and hand over a month's salary for the privilege of warbling some Frank Sinatra and being rewarded with a bowl of sliced fruits. (The uncomfortable scenario played out again a few years ago in the basement of the old Paramount Hotel in the East Coast. Desperate for business in a dying mall awaiting closure, a couple of girls in towering stilettos tottered after me in a scene from *March of the Penguins*. Rather scared, I ran out into the street and didn't look back. I can't see a penguin now without thinking of those poor girls.)

But I was intrigued to discover who was winning the battle for Balestier between old and new Singapore. Since I last visited, the gentrification process had begun. History had attracted the hipsters, drawn to the funky shophouses and the smell of skinny flat white cappuccinos. (As someone who has never drunk coffee and remains oblivious to its endless variations, I will always remember the first time I heard a friend order "a skinny flat white" in Australia. I expected him to be served Kate Moss.)

When I turned off Thomson Road and wandered into Balestier Road, new condos pockmarked the historic landscape in just about every direction. That development was startling. I was equally surprised to be greeted by a National Heritage Board (NHB) information panel. The map highlighted an excellent heritage trail, which I duly followed. I couldn't believe the street's transformation. Balestier's blue-collar crowd, construction workers and street hustlers had seemingly been swept away, replaced by affluent foreigners, mostly Caucasians. There were *ang mohs* everywhere. That didn't bother me. Some of my best family members are *ang mohs*. But the presence of an international community was an obvious indication of Balestier's steady shift from sleepy to swinging.

I found the crossroads, literally and culturally, at Zhongshan Park, a modern, typically glassy mixed-use development that jumped out at me. In a bid to incorporate history and high-rise, the project is called a park (there are some Banyan trees) and has a pond and a pretty timber walkway that leads to the Sun Yat Sen Nanyang Memorial Hall. But really, Zhongshan Park is a landscaped plaza dwarfed by a couple of hotels, an office tower and the ubiquitous shopping mall, and wouldn't look out of place in Manhattan or Manchester. It just looked out of place in Balestier. Judging by the packed restaurant on the left and a bustling bar filled with international clientele on the right, Zhongshan Park is destined for success. I spotted a menu offering dishes for brunch. Once the brunch brigade descend upon a local community, its annexation is inevitable. The air-kissers are coming. Their omnipresence is a jarring by-product of New Singapore. I was recently invited to (yet another) arty-farty café and, feigning politeness, asked how the tea party host had discovered the place.

"Well," she began. "You know how hard it can be to find that really good brunch place in Singapore…"

It certainly keeps me awake at night.

So Balestier is on the brink. The boutique hotels, bland office blocks and fun pubs are muscling in on the street, literally overshadowing the vintage shops, traditional family businesses and Chinese baroque shophouses that no doubt attracted the newcomers to the area in the first place. Old Balestier lives on. It's just tougher to find. But I found what I was looking for in the end.

I passed the splendid, eclectic shophouses where the roads of Balestier and Kim Keat meet in search of a world first. In 1927, the first airplane with a paying customer landed in Singapore. According to the NHB, newspaper tycoon W Van Lear touched down in a single-engine monoplane – to refuel – after flying in from Holland. He landed in Balestier Plain, a green field squeezed between the roads of Balestier, Tessensohn, Rangoon and Moulmein. Daft, eccentric history always appeals so I ventured into the underpass beneath the Central Expressway and asked an Indian guy for directions.

"Excuse me, do you live around here, in Balestier?" I began, far too breezily.

"Yah," he replied cautiously.

"Oh great. I'm looking for this plane, well not a plane, well it is a plain, it's Balestier Plain because there was this… Anyway, I'm looking for a grass field somewhere around here. I know it's late now and the field is probably dark, but I might as well go while I'm here. Could you show me where the field is, please?"

I thought he was going to run away. His face froze. Only later, when recounting the conversation with my wife, did I appreciate that a tall, sweaty, fast-talking white man had stopped an oblivious middle-aged Indian chap carrying his dinner in a dimly lit underpass and asked to be chaperoned towards a dark field.

"I don't know which field," he mumbled finally.

"Yah, it's called Balestier Plain, very historic. I know it's around here somewhere."

"Over there got a grass field," he said quickly, ushering me out of the underpass.

"That must be the one, thanks very much," I gushed, eager to continue the conversation to further express my gratitude. "So which block do you stay?"

"Er, follow that road, inside got one field."

And he was gone. But I followed his simple directions and found Balestier Plain. To my delight, there was a panel describing the world's first paid-passenger stop and roughly marking the spot where the plane landed in 1927. But there's only so long one can loiter alone in a park staring at a patch of grass without looking disturbed so I retraced my steps and returned to Balestier Road for an actual taste of Old Singapore.

SWEETLANDS Confectionary & Bakery has stood at the quiet corner of Kim Keat Lane and Kim Keat Close for more than 50 years. The family-run business churns out thousands of loaves and cakes every day. They bake around the clock to deliver across the island in no-frills, label-free bags. Nothing says traditional Balestier more than one of Sweetlands' buns. I turned down Kim Keat Road and passed a gym called De Boutique Gym, complete with French preposition, a grammatical reminder of the area's transformation (the use of French in an establishment's name that isn't French, doesn't sell anything French or share an association with anything remotely Gallic is right up there with "ye olde shoppes". Yes, I'm still looking at you, Marina Bay Sands).

I resisted the temptation to call the gym to see if anyone answered, "Hello, this is the De Boutique Gym" and strolled down the dark and rather dingy Kim Keat Lane, which was bordered by the backs of some scruffy shophouses. The smell pulled me towards Sweetlands. The bright yellow shop sign was possibly the only label on the property, with the busy bakery resembling a mini-factory rather than a shop. Hundreds of loaves were stacked floor to ceiling on crates and cakes were laid out across the tables as workers busied themselves tidying and stacking and pulling out more trays from a large, archaic oven. I picked up a cream bun and handed it to a jovial Chinese auntie.

"Hello, this is Sweetlands, right?" I asked rhetorically, just happy to chat.

"Again?" she shouted back.

"This is Sweetlands?"

She shook her head. "Sorry. English can?"

What a bloody cheek.

"I am speaking English, sort of," I mumbled. "This is Sweetlands, famous place in Balestier, Sweetlands, right?"

"Yah, yah, Sweetlands," she confirmed, satisfied with the successful translation of my English into English.

But her cream bun was something else. Every mini-mart bun since has tasted stale in comparison. Lighter than air, it soon vanished. Sweetlands is a taste of old Balestier, Old Singapore even. On my way back, I passed the gymnasium of New Singapore once more and ogled some remarkably buff men and women running on treadmills and doing squats near the window. Their glute workouts were impressive. But I preferred the buns at Sweetlands.

Somewhere on Balestier Plain, Singapore's first paying passenger landed on 29 June 1927. He was American W Van Lear Black, who thought he was a wealthy man until he saw the property prices and left.

Never mind the nearby gyms with fancy names, Sweetlands Bakery produces the best buns in Singapore.

Three

FOR SOME SINGAPOREANS, Mustafa Centre is the durian of shopping malls. You either love it or you hate it. Mentioning its name does not typically trigger a benign shrug of the shoulders and a sense of mild indifference. There is no middle ground with Mustafa. It's usually adoration or abhorrence. People swear by the place. Or people swear about the place. I've met plenty of both.

Of course, no one disputes the mall's success story. Indian businessman Mustaq Ahmad opened Mustafa in 1971, when the store essentially sold clothing, and eventually moved it to the ground floor of Serangoon Plaza in 1985. In the ensuing years, the department store expanded through Syed Alwi Road like an unstoppable selling machine, filling the street with floors of the strangest, weirdest collection of goods since Willy Wonka opened his chocolate factory. Mustafa remains a fixed point in Singapore's fluid, fickle shopping scene; a retail success story of survival in a voracious environment. From the outside, the mall defines the modern city. Step inside, however, and Old Singapore leaps from every dusty shelf. It's a time machine of tat.

Perhaps that's why Mustafa polarises. Some friends champion the shopping centre and its eclectic range. Others wouldn't be seen dead in the place (which is a shame because Mustafa does a fine range of black funeral suits on a budget). Some of the comments I've heard range from the funny and ignorant to the stupid and grotesque. *"Mustafa cannot go alone, got too many Indians... Mustafa very smelly one. Mustafa very expensive, Chinatown much better, got more choice..."*

What is really being implied is, Chinatown has better Chinese choices. Subconsciously or otherwise, Mustafa criticisms are tinged with the whiff of racial hegemony. After picking me up in Jalan Besar, a well-meaning taxi driver once said: "Mustafa OK for you, I pick up lots of foreign passengers outside Mustafa. But Mustafa not so good for Singaporeans." Presumably all those Indians who flock to the place are flown in from Mumbai then.

On other occasions, I've had fabulous conversations with Chinese taxi drivers who honestly had no idea that Mustafa has a greater range of groceries than, say, FairPrice or Cold Storage and is often cheaper (it's only a matter of time before Cold Storage rebrands itself as the exorbitant supermarket of choice for expats, tai tais, SPGs and anglophiles with the slogan, "you want it, we'll import it and triple the price". I'm convinced kindergarten kids randomly scribble numbers with crayons to set Cold Storage prices. And The Market Place should be renamed The Mortgage Place).

One taxi driver was stunned to learn that Mustafa sold bread, as if we had both stumbled into a Biblical famine. Another Chinese guy picked me up and gave me a neat potted history of Mustaq Ahmad's idea-to-empire story. (I must stress at this juncture that if I'm beginning to sound like one of those insufferable expats whose only interaction with Singaporeans comes from taxi drivers and bar staff, then try walking along Jalan Besar with a dozen Mustafa shopping bags in the midday sun before catching a bus opposite Sim Lim Square. People have died in less hazardous circumstances. And don't even think about dragging that many shopping bags past the other passengers on a No. 48 bus. They'll kill you.)

Still, Mustafa does itself no favours. The retailing giant has an almost pathological distrust of its own customers.

I squeezed my way through the Friday night crowd on Syed Alwi Road and was stopped outside one of Mustafa's many entrances. As always, a security guard took my bag and tied the zips together with one of those white plastic fasteners that are quick and easy to slide on, but require a pair of garden shears to remove. This process supposedly minimises the risk of shoplifting. But a Mustafa gatekeeper once tied a plastic fastener across the cover on my tennis racquet. Now, I'm no expert thief. My brief shoplifting career came to an abrupt end at the age of 10, when an elderly busybody of a shopper spotted me trying to put a Cadbury Crème Egg down my shorts and suggested I put it back. But what could I possibly slip between a tennis racquet and its cover? A frozen roti prata?

The only shopping security experience more preposterous than Mustafa's is the Kmart routine in Australia. Visit any of the chain's suburban behemoths and a ruddy-cheeked woman, invariably called Judy, will ask to check bags – at the store's entrance. After five years enduring this minor harassment, I was none the wiser to the purpose of the exercise beyond satisfying Judy's fetish for rummaging around other peoples' bags. A customer was never frog-marched to the manager's office saying: "Yeah, nah, Judy. I'm on the bones of me arse. Haven't got a pot to piss in. So I thought I'd help the billion-dollar Kmart out by sneaking all me worldly goods into the store, Judy. Yeah, nah."

As Mustafa's security guard busied himself tying up my rucksack, I asked if shoplifting was an ongoing concern at the store.

"Of course," he said cheerily, far too pleased that neither he nor his uniformed comrades were doing their jobs properly.

Now, much has already been made of the 300,000 items that Mustafa sells across its four levels in a building that spans 400,000 square feet. But it's the surreal placement and positioning of those 300,000 items that makes Mustafa more of a dreamscape than a department store. It's a shopping experience based on the scribbled shorthand of Lewis Carroll. I wandered in and stopped between a couple of shelves and, within touching distance, I could put my hands on a digital watch, a pack of Merlion keyrings, a pair of outsized headphones and an eyelash curler. That's not a logical, sensible, sellable display of items at a prime site by a store's entrance. That's the deranged work of an anarchic, Tourette's Syndrome-suffering shelf stacker, randomly ripping open cardboard boxes with a rusty Stanley knife and shouting: "OK, then what should go next to my Merlions… Fuck, headphones… And next to those we'll have… fuck, watches… and then maybe some… fuck, eyelash curlers."

Retail research must be negligible at Mustafa. There's a bewildering, but strangely refreshing, indifference to shopping norms and traditions. A rebellious streak runs through every aisle, with madcap gatherings of unconnected items all thrown together in nonsensical fashion. Customer surveys are presumably quaint, unnecessary forms to be filled in by conformist competitors. Unless, of course, Mustafa happened to survey a couple of tourists in dire need of the time, lots of Merlion keyrings, the latest headphones to listen to some banging tunes and anything that could tame the caterpillars above their eyelids.

Visit Mustafa and play the game for yourself. Hunt down the most peculiar scenes, the most disturbing gathering of household items and the most inhospitable public toilets. As I Botoxed my own face squeezing through the narrow aisles, I spotted pearl necklaces opposite torches; Scottish fruit and lemon biscuits beside Mickey Mouse schoolbags; children's party decorations next to sunglasses and, a personal favourite, bottles of plant fertiliser across the aisle from plastic toilet seats, as if the shelf stackers were in on a private scatological joke.

The gold jewellery section had the shiniest, tackiest, chunkiest necklaces and chains this side of Mr. T's bedside table. In the chocolate section, there was the widest range of tourism souvenirs – from London. Glow-in-the-dark Merlions kept Big Ben statues company on the same shelf. In one of the many clothes sections, I bumped into an adorable Malay kid trying on a black suit and tie, looking like a Reservoir Pup auditioning for *Bugsy Malone*. In the car section – yes, there's a car section – a handwritten sign read "steering wheel cover – only for car" just in case an unwitting customer bought one and stretched it across his new plastic toilet seat.

And the staff's helpfulness is second to none. In the telco section, there was a sign above a phone counter that read: "CCTV and spy gadget." Yes, that final 's' was missing, along with any sense of irony. I meandered over to a member of staff leaning over the glass counter and fiddling with a second-hand Nokia the size of a surfboard, and asked: "You sell spy gadgets? What kind of spy gadgets?"

"Don't know, not my section," he replied gruffly, not looking up from the prehistoric phone (if there was a market for two tin cans tied to a piece of string, Mustafa would have them stretched out beside the eyelash curlers).

"Oh, I see. So do the spy gadgets have any exploding pens?"

"Not my section," he repeated. "Come back when night shift starts."

Perhaps the shoe section best illustrated the shopping mall in all its unkempt glory. It wasn't so much a display as it was a jumble sale of shoes stacked on top of each other with less care than the church fetes of my childhood. Hundreds, possibly thousands, of pairs of shoes were piled metres high, with heels facing outwards in no discernible order. For a store compelled to identify its spy gadgets, there were few signs to be found among the bundles of shoes, boots, trainers and slippers. So I stopped a shelf stacker.

"Excuse me," I muttered. "How do I find the right size?"

"Look in the shoe."

And he wandered off, clearly not amused by my plainly stupid question.

But that's Mustafa. It isn't like any other shopping mall and makes no apologies for its oddities.

With soul-stripping predictability, New Singapore opens one dull, glassy temple to materialism after another. Every retail development promises an original experience and usually comes with an asinine theme seemingly conjured in a primary school classroom. (It's a rainforest! It's a sports stadium! A track runs around it! A river runs through it!) But like the Dagenham council houses of my childhood, they all look the same. Pull back the rooftop playgrounds and the water features and all that remains are empty shells filled with American coffees and Junior Whoppers and myopic landlords charging too much rent (which ensures that the only products guaranteed to survive are the American coffees and Junior Whoppers). These shopping centres feel about as authentically Singaporean as the imported items they sell. Few shoppers look particularly happy, but they shuffle through the boring buildings nonetheless.

Mustafa is hardly a charitable enterprise and its entire range is mostly purchased beyond the island's borders. But the mad mall is messy, unpredictable and, most of all, uniquely local. It's as familiar as fish head curry and offers an eclectic mix to rival rojak. There is little that feels uniform, sedate or contrived in Mustafa; a bit like Old Singapore.

And it sells spy gadgets. You'll probably find them next to the eyelash curlers.

WHEN I THINK of Rochor Centre, I think of a dead man. At least, I thought he might be dead. It was a Sunday afternoon and I was heading to a Jalan Besar studio to record a podcast when I discovered this chap laying face down on the pavement in front of Rochor Centre, opposite Fu Lu Shou Complex. He wasn't moving. The area was a hive of scurrying shoppers, but he was ignored. In fact, a few people were quickly stepping around him. He was a pathetic heap of a man, but a sadly neglected one. I crouched beside him and tapped his shoulder nervously. I had never touched a corpse before. But if he suddenly rolled over, pointed me towards a hidden camera and declared that I'd been punked, I might have killed him.

Eventually, he growled and turned onto his side, revealing eyes redder than the burning fires of Riau's peat bogs.

"Yeah?" he shouted, like he was taking my pizza order.

"Are you OK? Are you hurt?" I asked. "You're lying on the pavement."

"Yeah, yeah, OK, OK," he stammered, rising unsteadily to his feet. "Got $2?"

His breath reeked of something cheap, pungent and potent.

"What's it for?" I enquired.

He smiled broadly. "Er, *makan*, yeah, *makan, makan*."

I gave him the $2, he offered me a kind of drunken salute, turned and staggered off along Rochor Road, swaying from side to side like a toddler on roller skates. Maybe the money was for roti prata. Maybe it wasn't. But enough people had ignored him for one day.

The same could be said for Rochor Centre. For years, I viewed the small, four-block housing estate in a way I might view acupuncture. I knew it existed, I accepted that it benefitted some people, but I had little use for it and was not particularly compelled to investigate any further. But then a public trend repeated itself in New Singapore, one that must be privately infuriating policymakers. First, the Government announced that Rochor Centre – a housing estate built in 1977 and a little shop-soiled after decades of being poked, prodded and manhandled in one of the island's busiest retail and commercial districts – was going to be demolished. The four blocks of housing and the antiquated shopping centre beneath had to give way for the future construction of the North-South Expressway some time after 2016. The compulsory acquisition would inconvenience almost 570 families and 190 retailers, but the eventual expressway would reduce the travel times of hundreds of thousands of commuters from north to south; the greatest happiness for the greatest number and all that other practical utilitarian stuff.

But damn if some Singaporeans weren't grateful.

Letter writers, bloggers, normative dreamers and heritage fantasists lamented the potential loss of another brick in the country's cultural wall, another link to the nation's past being heartlessly removed. In such instances, it's hard not to picture the decision makers slapping their foreheads and asking: "Why do they want to live in the past? Why can't they crunch the numbers? Why is there a sleeping drunk on Rochor Road?"

So I found myself drawn towards Rochor Centre. And sure enough, I climbed the stone steps and ventured into a world that even most Singaporeans had left behind. There were no escalators, at least that I could see, leading to the shops on the upper floors. Residents had to use their own legs and everything. Confused children stood at the first step, holding the bannister and glancing around in horror, unable to fathom why they were not moving upwards in an orderly fashion. The place was frayed around the edges and locked in a time warp, similar perhaps to the Bras Basah Complex and its terrific second-hand bookstores. Simple family businesses spanning the generations dominated, with the usual hardware stores and CD shops selling what were clearly pirated Chinese albums with photocopied covers. Wandering past the mostly deserted shops and shuttered outlets, I could almost hear the death rattle.

Or it might have just been phlegm.

Now, nostalgia can be a problem. It's the opiate of the heritage romantics and I am hopelessly addicted. A constant yearning for 'the good old days' is unrealistic and unhelpful (and perhaps tainted by an inaccurate, whimsical view of what the 'good old days' really were). Rochor Centre provided an unwelcome jolt to the senses. The condemned buildings bluntly pointed out that if you want the rainbows of the good old days, you've got to put up with the spitting.

'Old-school' folks mostly populated the place. And they were compelled to relieve themselves of excess mucus more often than a Premier League footballer. A Chinese woman, in her late 70s, spat across the tiled floor like a tattooed gangster. Unimpressed with her initial effort, she unleashed a guttural, heaving roar from the darkest, dankest cavities at the back of her throat, making a distinct, primeval sound that could only be replicated by dropping a fridge on Chewbacca's foot. What she produced might have raised the water level in the Rochor Canal. For her coup de grace, she did that professional footballer thing of pushing in one nostril to turn the other into a fireman's hose. A quick blow on either side and she was finally satisfied that her nasal cavity was empty and the drain over which she was standing was full. At least she was a civic-minded soul. She found a drain first. Another resident was less respectful of his environment. Sitting outside a shop and reading a newspaper, he took a long drag on a cigarette, coughed up and fired a ball of phlegm that splattered across the tiles and just missed my feet. He sucked on the cigarette a second time and returned to his newspaper. Public spitting devotees have very much gone the way of non-air-conditioned buses in Singapore. You rarely see them any more. But their legacy lives on in Rochor Centre, along with foul public amenities.

I'm sure you are familiar with that cultural paradox left over from Old Singapore – i.e. the filthier the public toilet the more you have to pay to use it.

Stop for a tinkle in one of New Singapore's swanky malls and one can empty a bladder to the soothing tunes of piped music and luxuriate in a plush world of marble tiles and automated efficiency. Toilets flush automatically. Tap sensors trigger squirts of water automatically. Wall machines dispense paper by the sheet automatically and hot air contraptions dry those hands automatically. (Being Singapore, it's only a matter of time before a local university designs a toilet that sucks loose stools from stubborn bowels. It's only a matter of time.)

And most of all, these swanky abodes are free.

But then there are the other public toilets that we prefer not to acknowledge. These toilets are like that uncle who picks his toenails and talks to himself at family gatherings. We know he's there but we pretend he isn't. These toilets make us growl at our children when they suddenly declare that the *hor fun* they just ate has cheated the digestive system and they must relieve themselves immediately and, no, they cannot wait until Daddy drags them to the nearest modern air-conditioned shopping mall (the same shopping mall, incidentally, that hypocritical Daddy is always ridiculing for being the physical embodiment of soulless capitalism and sheep-bleating consumerism). They need to poo poo now. They need to use the worst public toilet that Old Singapore has to offer. They need to use a public toilet so horrid, so unclean and so nose-meltingly dreadful that the place employs an auntie to charge us a bloody admission fee.

Well, I found one at Rochor Centre.

Sitting on a rickety chair behind a table, the auntie had her coins all laid out on the table, mimicking a celluloid bank robber counting out his ill-gotten gains. The sign said 10 cents. I handed her a 20 cent coin. She shot me a withering look that detailed her thoughts on the matter. *Don't even think about asking for change, ang moh.* The smell hit me before I passed through the turnstile. Scientists claim that only cockroaches will survive a nuclear holocaust. So could this smell. I'm neither squeamish nor a snob (a stomach illness once left me so incapacitated and at the mercy of erratic bowel movements that I filled a dustbin on a London railway station. I'm no stranger to depravation). But Rochor Centre was beyond my hardened senses. I found myself peeing with one hand and shielding my nose with the other. Rotten timber and cracked tiles surrounded me. Years of decay stained the walls and floors. A couple of small cockroaches crawled across the wall above the urinal, which added to the ambience and also suggested that if a nuclear holocaust had just taken place, my theory had been successfully tested. I pushed the flush. Not a great deal happened. The smell was making me retch. Remember the "world's worst toilet" Ewan McGregor stumbled upon in *Trainspotting*? Rochor Centre had borrowed the set design. Had I died at the urinal – and further exposure made that a distinct possibility – I'm not sure anyone would've noticed.

I hurried back through the turnstile, still shielding my nose for melodramatic effect and ensuring I registered my non-verbal complaint with the 10 cent-hoarding auntie. She could hardly care less. But Singaporeans should. This isn't about snobbery, but basic public decency. Building artificial gardens for tourists and eco-friendly waterways for young families are fine initiatives, but let's not neglect older residents and communities. Rochor Centre's departing families may miss their old homes, but not the primitive, Third World public amenities that lie beneath. All Singaporeans deserve better.

And this is less than half of Mustafa Centre.

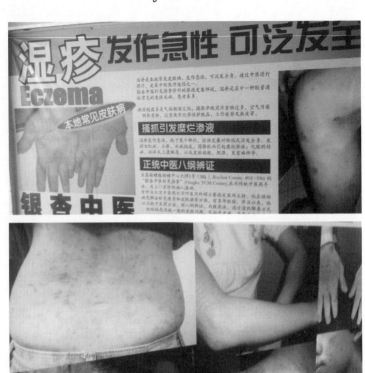

When Rochor Centre goes, the old school marketing posters will go with it. And who agreed to be the models for the Rochor Centre clinic posters?

Four

SECONDHAND MARKETS reveal so much about a country's culture. Australians, for example, throw away nothing. DIY is in their DNA. Weekends are spent building outdoor decking areas the size of a three-room flat and weekdays are spent paying master craftsmen to repair the botched outdoor decking. To their immense credit, Australians recycle and reuse just about everything, partly because they endure a harsh environment and suffer the direct consequences of their carbon footprints. But it's mostly because they are tight-arses. Garage sales are the inevitable extension of such a thrifty mentality. In a nutshell, suburbanites open up their garages, fill them with shit and then invite friends, neighbours and strangers over to buy it. I was once standing at the counter of my old Australian optician when a guy walked in and asked if his sunglasses could be repaired. He dumped some plastic bits on a table. An archaeologist could not have pieced his sunglasses back together. When gently informed that his sunglasses were, indeed, no longer sunglasses but a pile of plastic crap, the shocked chap shook his head ruefully and said: "Yeah, I knew it. Typical of our modern throwaway culture, eh? Guess these will be going in the next garage sale, mate." Imagine what the landfill at Pulau Semakau looks like when it receives

600 tonnes of non-incinerable waste every day. Now imagine an Aussie fella sticking some into a plastic bag and saying: "Got some bloody good compost here mate, five bucks, bloody bargain. I'll even throw in some broken bits of sunglasses for ya." That's an Australian garage sale.

Where I grew up in Dagenham, England, secondhand markets were commonly known as car boot sales. They were less popular than the Australian garage sales, due in large part to the latent snobbery of the working classes. Certainly in my household, there was a benign request from my mother to "stop buying that secondhand shit. You'll have everyone thinking we haven't got a pot to piss in". Anything deemed broken, old-fashioned or out-of-date was sent to "the tip". (The tip wasn't a refuse collection centre but a patch of wasteland behind the local library. But it served the same purpose. And more kids hung out at the tip than in the library.)

In Singapore, of course, no one has anything old or secondhand. Electronic devices and mobile phones are bought and then upgraded a week later because a newer model with a 3D map of Nauru and a blinking light has been launched. We can be defined by what we keep and what we throw away.

All of which helps to explain why I adore Thieves Market.

I walked briskly around the dusty building site of the future Downtown MRT line, dodged the diggers making a mess of Jalan Besar and passed the snaking lanes carved out with temporary fencing to reach the market with the fabulous name. Thieves Market has been tucked away behind Jalan Besar since the 1930s and was once a place to fence stolen goods. Now it's one of the island's most entertaining flea markets. A hoarder's paradise, it may sell relatively new items thrown out by impatient Singaporeans, older goods like the sort usually found hanging out of the back of a Ford Escort boot in a muddy Essex field, or even the plainly useless junk occasionally spread out across the concrete floor of an Australian garage. I have never come across so many things that I didn't want or that I couldn't live without anywhere else.

I arrived at 1pm on a Saturday afternoon just as the market vendors were laying out old rugs, tarpaulins and even bed stands to display their weird wares. Extra plastic sheets and old coffee shop parasols were then tied to the corrugated fencing lining the market to provide merciful shade. By 2pm, bargain hunters had flooded the narrow side streets. They came in all shapes, sizes, colours and ages to have a little fun filtering the junk from any nuggets of treasure. Sunburnt backpackers marvelled at a rare, authentic Singaporean experience. Old timers sifted through the hundreds of watches stuffed in cardboard boxes. And construction workers haggled over the price of second-hand trainers (those invisible folks who empty our rubbish chutes and build our homes were very visible here).

Being something of an experienced connoisseur when it comes to buying what my mother refers to as "a load of old shit", I positively frolicked in the mountains of mess and the benign chaos. Everyone was shouting, haggling and arguing, but it was always playful. The noise was incessant but never in that stultifying drone that fills cavernous malls thanks to over-eager salesmen waffling on about credit card specials in dodgy American accents.

And it was mostly English. That was the commonly heard language. At first, the familiarity was jarring. I walked around the market several times to check it wasn't a coincidence, but most conversations between vendors and customers were conducted in English and sometimes Malay. There was a smattering of Mandarin and Hokkien, but the most common languages were those that united the wonderfully diverse crowd. The older vendors relied mostly on English to engage with their Western and South Asian customers – and with each other. The warmth and sincerity among the vendors really was quite wonderful. It's impossible for me to say if such friendly camaraderie existed among market traders and their daily clientele in Old Singapore. I wasn't there. But it certainly doesn't exist in today's shopping malls.

The crowd's diversity was matched by the distinct lack of homogenous products. Few vendors, if any, offered a distinct range of goods. They sold whatever they had gotten their hands on. Nothing conformed, very little actually made much sense. One vendor had a doll of South Korean pop star Psy in a *Gangnam Style* pose beside a rusty military bugle. I had to walk away. I was seriously considering buying that bugle. There were clocks, watches, shoes, clothes, playing cards, vinyl records, VCR players, CDs, cassette tapes, phones and phone cables, TVs, shot glasses, repaired fans and rice cookers, Buddha statues, Buddhist amulets and laser discs among the collection of diverse and surreal products large enough to fill this chapter. The laser discs caught my eye. I have never bought one, nor have I ever owned a laser disc player, but someone was selling a *Pulp Fiction* disc with an attractive cover. I called out to the burly uncle, who was sitting under an umbrella in a white vest and slippers and eating *nasi lemak*.

"Hey, the discs, how much ah?"

"$2 each one," he said, scooping up a spoonful of ikan bilis. "You buy all, I give you special price."

"No, I just want this one," I said, holding up *Pulp Fiction.*

"Ah, that one very nice show," he replied, nodding his head with the authority of the late Roger Ebert.

"You seen it?"

"No. But the guy say very good. He sell me $1 each. I sell you $2, enough already."

I pointed at a dusty, electronic contraption sandwiched between many others on top of a crate. "Is that a laser disc player?"

"Yah, only $20."

"That's cheap."

"Yah. Might not work one."

"It's broken?"

"Don't know. Guy sell me from his car this morning, stop outside, no time to check one. But can clean head, never mind. I don't bluff you one OK. I buy $15. I sell you $20, five dollars enough already."

"But it doesn't work?"

"Yah, maybe."

I enjoyed the sales pitch, but even I draw the line at buying things that do not work. Still, Thieves Market was an uplifting place. It was an adrenaline rush of nostalgia, a quick shot of living history. But the flea market sat in the shadow of its potential executioner. Vendors attached their green tarpaulin roofs to a fence that divided two worlds. Construction workers, no doubt the same guys who flocked to Thieves Market for cheap trainers and phones, were digging and tunnelling their way along the new Downtown line. MRT trains will soon hurtle through subterranean Jalan Besar. Maybe Thieves Market will survive the eventual opening of Jalan Besar station. Maybe it won't. I'd like to think there'll be enough room left when the station is finished to throw down some tatty blankets and sell *Gangnam Style* dolls and rusty military bugles.

Two hours later, in a fit of blind panic, I ran back to the stall and bought the *Pulp Fiction* laser disc.

All I need now is a laser disc player.

AFTER THE delightful Thieves Market, I struggled with the middle-class metamorphosis of Jalan Besar. One of Singapore's oldest streets was turning into another cupcake corner. I have nothing against cupcakes, of course. I grew up stuffing my face with the chocolatey treats in the name of charity, buying dozens of them at primary school fundraisers organised for Bob Geldof's Live Aid. (Those African kids have no idea how many 10p bakes I bought for them. I hope they appreciate the sacrifice.) But the cupcakes were baked and sold for a good cause – if the class raised enough money, we wouldn't have to hear *Do They Know It's Christmas* any more. They were not pulled from the oven to accommodate Jalan Besar's affluent overspill from the CBD.

When I think of gentrification, I think of an offbeat chapter of my childhood spent at the Old Spitalfields Market in East London. Spitalfields was one of the world's most historic markets. King Charles had granted a licence for fresh produce to be sold on the site in 1638. Jack the Ripper stalked its darkened streets in 1888. And generations of my family bought and sold stolen goods there. I'm not suggesting those events are connected, but I was thrown into the intoxicating working-class world of the Old Spitalfields Market as an impressionable teenager. My uncle gave me a part-time, overnight job as a labourer, climbing into container trucks to remove pallets of exotic fruits and vegetables from obscure African countries. During my brief stint, I was offered pirated videos, discounted drugs and given advice on everything from fencing stolen goods to finding the best sex in London – all in a single night.

The market moved to a new location in the 1990s and severed those deeply entrenched working-class roots that had taken hold through the centuries. When I returned to the Old Spitalfields Market a couple of years ago, it looked like a Richard Curtis movie set, depicting that mythical, middle-class London of potpourri, leather satchels and vintage jewellery that seems popular with movie-goers. I half expected Hugh Grant and Keira Knightley to pop out in matching scarves and ask for directions to the Parisian cheese stall. The place was filled with Asian tourists in woolly hats and gloves (in June) rummaging through the handcrafted bric-a-brac.

And that's when the working-class chip on the shoulder inevitably pokes through. If an Amazonian tribe is at risk of being left homeless by deforestation, anthropologists quite rightly fall over themselves to champion indigenous rights and fight for the preservation of native culture. When it's an urban working-class community threatened by gentrification, on the other hand, the estate agents move in and poorer families and businesses are forced out. In such prime, central locations, those baristas and cupcake bakers need the space.

In the gentrification race, Jalan Besar sits somewhere between Balestier, which is barely out of the starting blocks and Tiong Bahru, which is breathlessly closing in on the finish line. It makes for a strange mix. There are the quieter, slower roads around Dunlop Street, which have a scruffy, relaxed charm, and the stunningly restored Kam Leng Hotel at the other end of Jalan Besar. The hotel was built in 1927 and designers have painstakingly stripped back the interior to its Nanyang core. Despite stiff competition from restored rivals (the curvy lines of Allenby House and the Sandpiper Hotel nearby stand out), Kam Leng Hotel is Jalan Besar's most tasteful torchbearer for Old Singapore.

Elsewhere, the battle between trendy and traditional is more bizarre. In a row of shophouses, a busy cupcake and coffee joint sits in the company of a car tyre and battery shop and a Chinese herbal soup outlet. Opposite Jalan Besar Stadium, a funky homemade pie shop does a roaring trade, despite being obscured by bamboo scaffolding. In a gentle corner of Tyrwhitt Street, the elegant Chye Seng Huat Hardware building hosts a coffee house so swinging, it doesn't even bother with any discernible signs. I opened the door and the general make-up, attire and jazzy vibe of the coffee house clientele all seemed to say the same thing. *You might be an ang moh, but don't even think about coming in here without at least wearing thick Buddy Holly glasses and a trilby hat.*

The old-world, local charms of the Berseh Food Centre and cheap roti prata were only a street away, but felt like they were in another time. From its swampland beginnings and slaughterhouses to its New World cabaret acts and boxing matches, Jalan Besar had always been a place where the labourer could feel like a king, the worker's weekend playground. But the alcohol ban following the Little India riot and the steady growth of bars, coffee houses and arts and craft shops were colluding to push out its pioneers.

Besides, themed cafes are not a guarantee of funkiness. There is the risk of the opposite happening, of Jalan Besar becoming just another hip haven, interchangeable with those found on the cobbled streets of Melbourne and London's Soho. Jalan Besar was already a funky town. The former swamp plain on the Rochor River has been drawing eclectic crowds since the 19th Century, but its target audience appears to be narrowing. The new, trendy menus do the maths. How many Singaporeans and foreign workers can afford a $5 cupcake?

Thieves Market makes you buy stuff you don't need. I recently bought an empty Eiffel Tower-shaped whiskey bottle there. I don't know why either.

Old and New Singapore collide at every corner on Jalan Besar. Note the cyclists going in opposite directions on the same side of the road. They just don't care here.

One of the highlights of Jalan Besar, Kam Leng Hotel has gotten a makeover that makes it genuinely attractive.

Five

I EXPERIENCED my first hawker centre when I was 11 years old. Only it wasn't a hawker centre, it was a greasy-spoon East London café in a decaying industrial heartland. But the food, atmosphere and clientele were essentially the same. Lots of unhealthy but tasty fried food was eaten. The air was coloured with that glorious sound of biting invective. There were rude words, bad words and sarcastic words – all of which came from my mother. Working with me in the family café, she flirted and argued with customers whilst smoking a cigarette in one hand and eating a fried sausage in the other. It left quite an imprint on a young boy's memory. It also left us low on sausages. She doesn't do any of the above any more. The local council knocked down the café years ago.

So I always struggled with the 'ang moh gets down with the heartlanders' tag that I was naively saddled with after my first Singapore book was published. The patronising association (to both me and the heartlanders) grated, suggesting that I was somehow walking on the wild side with the working classes by fraternising with the local commoners at hawker centres. If anything, the opposite applied. Hawker centres came across as sedate affairs after 10 years of working in a family café where security came in the shape of a wooden truncheon with the words "Spanish aspirin" scrawled across it. The truncheon was kept beneath the counter and I was ordered to use it to whack any red-eyed Irish labourers who argued over the prices. If I really wanted to hurt them, I served them a stronger cup of stewed tea.

Working-class eateries flowed through my DNA long before I arrived in Singapore. Hawker centres helped to reinforce the relationship. They say you never forget your first hawker centre love and Chicken Rice Killer was my first. Chicken Rice Killer never greeted customers at his Toa Payoh stall without a bloodied chopper in his hand and an apron covered in the fresh entrails of a still quivering corpse lying on the hosed-down floor behind him. He always had a drippy-looking partner working over his shoulder, who presumably disposed of all the bodies. He just grinned inanely and chopped things, usually pelvises and femurs. Before serving me, Chicken Rice Killer would shout to his friend: "Eh, pass me the chopper. No, that one ah, the one with the blood, I scare the shit out of the *ang moh*."

So I love hawker centres. Like National Service, they are great social levellers. Rich and poor sit side by side, armed only with packets of tissue to *chope* seats. When I worked at my family's café, I was always struck by the social juxtaposition of suited and booted company bosses sitting beside the folks from the factory floor. It was probably the only time of the day their paths crossed. From East London to Singapore's heartlands, cheap, good food bridges the income gap.

And I was looking for the man who had helped to build that relationship here by playing a considerable part in shaping the Singapore hawker centre.

Seow Poh Leng was a remarkable Singaporean for several reasons. Born in 1883, he became a successful banker, a passionate patron of the arts, an advocate for pioneering public works and an extremely generous philanthropist. Most of all, he championed the common man, his tireless work best exemplified by the Hawker Bill in 1931. When it came to hawkers in the early 20th Century, authorities often closed one eye (luckily, they're not accused of doing that any more). Hawkers were looked down upon by colonials and accused of being a public nuisance and a bit of an unsightly rabble for those seeking to enjoy tiffin at Raffles Hotel after a hard day sitting beneath a shaded rickshaw. Seow took up the hawkers' cause with a missionary's zeal. He highlighted how out of touch the elite was to the demands of poorer Singaporeans (this seems eerily familiar); how the masses' culinary needs were just as important as those of the wealthy (again, there's a certain similarity); and how there had to be a delicate social balance between the choices of rich and poor (now it's just spooky).

Seow met with the Hawker Bill committee. He wrote many newspaper articles in support of the 'hapless hawker' (in publications presumably read by colonials, which must have made him less popular than a fart in a lift). He never stopped fighting for the less fortunate. So I was eager to find his family home in a famous street that I had previously ignored.

I left Somerset MRT and passed Orchard Gateway. To be honest, I'd rather pass a kidney stone. My first three years in Singapore were spent working on the fifth floor of the demolished Specialist Shopping Centre and yet I rarely know where I am in the endlessly changing labyrinth of lost shoppers. Puzzled visitors can be spotted at the traffic lights beside Emerald Hill Road, holding street maps and muttering: "Where the fuck are we?"

And they're Singaporeans.

But after leaving Orchard Road's cacophonous din of construction site drillers, I heard something startling. With every step, the unsettling noise got louder. It was unfamiliar, disorienting and alien. It was the sound of birds. Emerald Hill was alive with the sound of musical birds. These were not the sounds of scavenging crows pecking away at leftover chicken wings on a coffee shop plate, but the chatter of orioles and other exotic birds feasting on the bottlebrush trees along one of Singapore's loveliest streets (and wealthiest, of course. I passed a chauffeur taking a nap in a cream-coloured Rolls Royce bigger than my apartment).

The sounds of nature and relative quiet so close to Orchard Road were entirely unexpected. As I crossed Hullet Road, I realised that I'd never ventured this far along Emerald Hill before. And the empty street suggested that I was not alone. Years ago, I had only two reasons to visit Emerald Hill. The first was to meet my wife when she previously taught at the international school there, and the second was to get into a bar argument with an inebriated Australian trying to put his hand up my wife's skirt.

The further I walked, the more peaceful Emerald Hill became. Its charm derives from its tranquillity. The terraced houses, many restored to their former Chinese baroque glory complete with hand-carved timber doors and tiled window arches, were an invigorating peek into Old Singapore. The stylish presence of the pioneering Peranakan Babas was everywhere. But the street's stillness was its real selling point. Being surrounded by blossoming trees, singing birds and butterflies was a more rewarding experience than being handed leaflets for discounted silver jewellery at the other end of the street. Many of the houses are protected. Naturally, I expected Seow's old abode to be an architectural gem.

Naturally, his house was gone.

He had worked for Lim Boon Keng. He married the great granddaughter of Tan Tock Seng. His second marriage produced a daughter, Rosie Seow Guat Kheng. And her daughter, Stella Kon, wrote the classic *Emily of Emerald Hill*. Their family home through much of this extraordinary period was called

Oberon – or No. 117 Emerald Hill Road. I was certain the property would be preserved. I discovered a swanky apartment complex, Residences at Emerald Hill, now occupied the site. If there was a heritage panel or plaque dedicated to the hawkers' champion, I didn't find it. New Singapore had won again. Not that the street craves or desires public sympathy. The URA has already gazetted many of the houses and if you fancy buying one, $10 million should do the trick. It's a wealthy, self-sufficient enclave, a world away from hawker centres. But the hawkers' champion of Emerald Hill is still worth remembering.

BACK IN THE HUBBUB of the island's premier shopping district, I wondered if I was being a tad harsh on Orchard's contribution to the country's heritage and its sense of national identity and collective belonging. So here are a few paragraphs on what the area offers to Old Singapore…

MOVING SWIFTLY ON, I trotted towards No. 38 Oxley Road. For the benefit of anyone not familiar with Singapore's Third World to First World narrative, No. 38 Oxley Road was where a policeman once ordered me to move along.

It was also Mr Lee Kuan Yew's family home.

By his own admission, Singapore's first prime minister was not a man prone to bouts of maudlin reflection. He had little patience for sentimentality. Before his death, he had made his feelings on the Oxley Road property clear. Eventually, the house should be demolished and the planning rules changed to increase the land value and maximise the area's profit.

But, if I may be so bold, Mr Lee was wrong. His modesty and unforgiving pragmatism cannot undermine the property's incomparable significance to the country. Modern Singapore was born in that house, where People's Action Party founders gathered to establish a political alternative to colonial masters. The island's future was shaped over warm beer and long lunches there. The current prime minster was raised there. It's a secluded, unfussy home, but one that shares political kinship with Peacefield in the United States. That historic home produced two national leaders – American Presidents John Adams and John Quincy Adams – and so did No. 38 Oxley Road. The Massachusetts homestead is now part of the Adams National Historical Park and has attracted hundreds of thousands of visitors from across the world. The Peacefield Stone Library has more than 14,000 personal papers and books that once belonged to the second and sixth American Presidents. If the Lee family home is torn down, ravenous real estate developers will move in.

Considering John Adams' role in helping to shape the Declaration of Independence and being one of the document's signatories, Peacefield was long ago added to the US National Register of Historic Places, guaranteeing its preservation. Despite

Mr Lee Kuan Yew's role in shaping Singapore's independence and being its first prime minister, the Oxley Road property could one day be a gleaming, functional condo with residents splashing through a snaking, eco-friendly, infinity pool.

The uncertain fate of the single most important family home in Singapore's history summarises the economic pragmatism of its environment. A Kinder Egg interpretation of history is often endorsed. There's an attractive, hollow shell – like the old Cathay cinema – with no substance within. It's shiny on the outside, but not particularly nourishing or sustaining. Information panels and National Heritage Board markers are helpful, but offer no physical connection. Old Singapore should be a tactile experience where possible. We should touch it.

Of course, I knew that was out of the question at No. 38. No one gets touchy-feely outside the Lee family house. No one gets to walk on that side of the road. Making my way up the street's steady incline, I peered into the other properties. I don't wish to speak disparagingly of other peoples' homes, but Oxley Road boasts some of the crumbliest, craggiest private service apartments in Singapore. Considering the street's proximity to Orchard Road and the exorbitant land value, the paint-chipped walls and rusty windows frames are screaming "en-bloc". Is it a security issue or to spare the influential neighbours a couple of years of industrial drilling? Either way, there was a strange, begrudging admiration for an international statesman so indifferent to his habitat. Asian leaders are so often guilty of building colossal, vulgar palaces and ostentatious family retreats to celebrate their omnipotence. Mr Lee wasn't one of them.

Walking briskly on the other side of Oxley Road, I passed the first road barrier – there was one on each side of the property – and stopped just before the second. I took a couple of photos. This did not go down well. The police officer stepped out of his circular security post and starting clapping at me, as if shooing a crow away from a hawker centre table.

"Eh, cannot take photos of this house ah," he shouted, firmly but not overly aggressively.

Rather entertainingly, his arms were fully outstretched as he clapped, making him an intriguing hybrid of Frankenstein's Monster and a performing seal. There was a temptation to throw a dead fish as part of a token feeding exercise.

"I'm sorry," I replied, in a pitiful attempt to play for time.

"Cannot take photos of this house."

The outrage consumed me. The veins in my forehead throbbed and knotted like snakes on a plane. I was on a public street, on the right side of the road and the right side of civil and personal liberties. This was an affront to my liberal sensibilities. I was going to challenge this box ticker, get his name, file a report, take his badge, pen indignant letters to the press, erupt on social media, write a blog, stage a sit-in protest and force this subservient individual to physically remove me. I would not be moved.

"Ah, OK, sorry."

I shit myself.

It's probably not the response you were looking for. I know I wasn't. I peered down and was as surprised as anyone to see my legs running away from each other. The sudden scurrying wasn't so much triggered by fear as it was by self-preservation. It was just a house. Only it wasn't. It was *his* house, instinctively commanding a profound respect and mild anxiety in equal measure. I wasn't petrified by the place. It was a sunny afternoon on Oxley Road not a *Nightmare on Elm Street*, but I was a tad dismayed by my cowardly reaction. The imposing stature of the man and his relatively humble abode are the reasons why it should still be preserved.

I retreated beneath a shady tree at the top of Lloyds Road, composed myself and fashioned a workable plan. I would be one of those freaky kids with photographic memories; the ones who catch a glimpse of the Manhattan skyline from an airplane window and then produce an identical facsimile in glorious watercolours. Forget the camera. I'd snap mental images. Taking a deep breath (I don't know why either, my melodrama was getting a little carried away), I returned to Oxley Road. In a puerile display of petty defiance, I offered the police officer a mock salute. I showed him. He ignored me. But I took in every detail, every architectural nuance and quirk, every camouflaging branch, twig and leaf. And I can say, with some authority, that old Singapore's most celebrated family home is a cream-coloured fortress. It was entirely obscured by dense foliage and a high wall with a police officer stationed on either side of the property to offer protection and no sense of humour.

Its owner wasn't sentimental, but other Singaporeans increasingly are. Mr Lee might have seen a dilapidated 19th Century building falling into disrepair. But the country's independent government was born in its basement. No. 38 Oxley Road must be saved. Incidentally, the bottom of the street was framed by a structure that may well symbolise New Singapore. Unlike No. 38, it was practical, maximised revenue and was entirely in keeping with the long-term plans of a hardheaded metropolis. It was an ERP gantry.

Six months after I visited, Mr Lee died. The unprecedented outpouring of public emotion showed that Singaporeans do care about such things. Photo essays of the property's simple, austere interior went viral. A petition was started, calling for the home to be gazetted. These things matter. No. 38 Oxley Road matters. It's not just a building. It's a birthplace. Shortly after the state funeral, I returned to the property to show it to my daughter. She asked if it had a garden. I said yes. She asked if she could move in. I said no. But she should one day be able to visit the historic home. Hopefully.

THE TEENAGE BOYS were distracting. As I tried to watch a marvellous, grainy documentary on the birth of Toa Payoh's housing estate, they kept fiddling with the phone. It was a black cradle telephone and a seemingly innocuous exhibit in our fake living room. The three of us were sitting in a recreated HDB flat from the 1970s, complete with period furniture and terrific analog TV in a wooden cabinet, in the basement of the National Museum of Singapore. The HDB flat was part of the Singapore 700 Years exhibition and, as a child besotted with the groundbreaking education series *How We Used To Live*, I was considering moving in. No matter how tacky, these reconstructions of yesterday's homes always fascinate. People's history is always the most personal, the most profound. And they always have strange gadgets to play with, like the cradle telephone.

"No lah, it's like this I tell you," I heard the skinny teenager say, pushing aside his tubbier friend.

They crouched over the retro coffee table and fiddled with the phone. Sitting at the other end of the traditional Chinese settee, I slapped a hand over my right ear and tried to focus on the extraordinary footage of Toa Payoh's swamp being cut down in the early 1970s.

"Please, I see before, OK," the tubby one interjected. "It's like this OK. You put your finger inside and push the number, like an iPhone."

I think I bit my tongue until it bled.

"No, I'm telling you, must put your finger inside and then turn the circle one," insisted the skinny one. "Then the phone can register the number."

"No need. Just put the finger inside and push. Like this."

I gave up on the Toa Payoh documentary and watched a Singaporean teenager, blessed by birthright with one of the world's finest educations, squeeze a stubby finger through one of the little circles on the telephone and press hard.

"You're kidding, right?" I heard myself say.

"What?" he wondered, as his bored friend skulked off to play on the old-fashioned children's roundabout (I'll get to that).

"You think you only have to stick your finger in one of the holes?" I asked, pointing at the dial on the phone.

"Yeah lah, it's a phone what," he shrugged, in that loud, patronising tone used to inform an elderly relative that it's bath time.

"No, I know it's a phone. But you can't just stick your finger in and... I mean... you have to actually turn... have you ever seen a phone like this before?"

"Of course, in old movies. But I never use before."

So for the benefit of the teenager, who in a few short years will be handed an automatic weapon and ordered to shoot stuff on Pulau Tekong, I demonstrated how to use a cradle telephone.

"You find the number you want, put your finger in and then turn the dial all the way around until it reaches the little metal arm and then you release it," I said, speaking and demonstrating slowly.

Wide-eyed, my new friend absorbed the high-tech presentation, nodding gently as he stared at the cutting-edge communicative contraption of its day, the iPhone of my early childhood.

"Each number must go all the way around the circle?" he asked finally.

"All the way around."

"Wah. So troublesome."

And he left to push his mate on the playground roundabout.

I could say that museums are a cheap, accessible portal to our past (the National Museum of Singapore is free for all citizens and permanent residents as all national museums should be). And Singapore's oldest museum is afforded the rare privilege of exhibiting history and being history. Its history can be traced to 1849 and there's no doubting its architectural elegance that successfully combines its Neo Palladian and Renaissance influences. The museum is worth visiting just for its tasteful displays of the Singapore Stone and William Farquhar's drawings (that man never stopped sketching, did he? No wonder Boat Quay went to pot so quickly. Illegal gambling haunts and opium dens were spreading like weeds along the Singapore River and the governor was at home colouring in his orchids).

I could say all of that about the National Museum of Singapore. Or I could just say that the place teaches teenagers how to use a cradle telephone. That's not being facetious or facile. On the contrary, Singapore's Blitzkrieg towards… towards… I'm not entirely sure what we're marching towards, but I know we keep marching… drags us further away from our predecessors. If we are unfamiliar with the workings of a phone found in almost every Singaporean household just a generation ago, what else are we forgetting, ignoring, losing in the thickening dust of urban renewal? Never mind the Singapore Stone, teenagers cannot identify with their parents' past. It's alien. They can't even phone home.

But the National Museum of Singapore is trying to plug Singaporeans back into their heritage grid. The sparse 700 Years exhibition might have taken a deliberately minimalist approach or was more likely an honest reflection of a country that has so few precious artifacts to call its own. The documentaries were the high point. The birth of Toa Payoh's housing estate was one and the other felt like an outtake from *Saint Jack*. Called

Singapore: Crossroads of the East, the black and white clip from 1938 revealed the most amazing footage from a spectacularly naïve British colony on the eve of World War II. While Hitler finalised his plans to goosestep into Poland, the Brits stiffened their upper lips and toasted their opulence on the verandah as a near-faceless local swept the mosaic tiles in the background. A remarkable showcase of life in Singapore, the clip also revealed shots of the Singapore River, the business district, the Fullerton and the Victoria Theatre, along with grinning colonials going about their business in the finest white linens whilst Singaporeans went about their menial tasks of unloading pallets on the docks, pulling rickshaws or directing traffic. But the plummy commentary was something else. Presumably holding his script in one hand and a pink gin in the other, the self-satisfied narrator strangled his vowels and said: "Unpretentious homes hosted popular tea and garden parties." The camera panned across a cluster of black and white bungalows as any number of Caucasian faces raised a glass to their imperial power. If such stately homes were considered unpretentious, heaven knows what the cinematographer thought of the kampongs.

The colonial smugness of the British upper classes on screen irritated me. Watching the *Downton Abbey* lookalikes celebrate their subjugation of a nation on the cushioned wicker chairs of Raffles Hotel, it was hard not to forget how, four years later, they were on the run – from an army on bicycles. The thought of Singapore's financial district and high-end residences and restaurants being dominated by cash-rich foreigners with no deep allegiance to the country now seems archaic and distasteful. Thank god that no longer happens, eh?

The museum's exhibition ended in that HDB living room in 1970s Toa Payoh, where a children's playground from yesteryear had been installed (by far the most child-friendly exhibit in the museum). No one was looking so I had a quick spin on the roundabout. Reluctantly, I had to stop when a young family wandered into the old living room. I expected the kids to make a dash for the roundabout, but they were instead drawn to the strange device on the coffee table, pawing at the black object like the apes bouncing around the monolith in *2001: A Space Odyssey.* I sighed and headed back to the cradle telephone. My work is never done.

Emerald Hill offers beautifully restored homes and no Orchard Road roadshows. It's just about perfect.

Look at the officer outside No. 38 Oxley Road. He couldn't take his eyes off me.

A glorious building, the National Museum of Singapore has decent exhibitions and a children's roundabout, as all museums should.

Six

AS WE PULLED OVER along Marina Coastal Drive, the frowning taxi driver made little effort to conceal his irritation. He peered through the passenger window at the day-trippers making their way towards Marina South Pier.

"Stop here for what?" he asked gruffly.

"We're going to Lazarus Island," my daughter cheerily replied, picking up her bucket and spade.

"Lazarus what?"

"Lazarus Island. It's next to St John's Island," I said.

"Ah," the taxi driver cried. "What for?"

"To have a look around, you know."

"St John's Island got nothing wha'."

"We just want to relax for a few hours," I added, shuffling along the back seat.

"Ah, I understand."

He didn't.

To my surprise, Marina South Pier was bustling with Singaporean families carrying picnics. There was also a healthy smattering of European backpackers and Asian domestic helpers and construction workers taking wefies with one another on a preciously rare day off (I made a point of not interacting with them, just in case they made me pregnant). The terminal replaced the iconic Clifford Pier in 2006 and this was the first time I had visited. In my naivety, I had expected a handful of eco-warriors and a pack of stray dogs trotting past the tumbleweed. But Marina South Pier buzzed with eager explorers (yes, St John's Island may be three kilometres away from the mainland, but in a country where homes, shopping malls, clinics, pre-schools and MRT stations are all stacked in a glassy, vertical prism, the island retreat might as well be in another dimension). I was excited by the prospect of savouring a slice of Old Singapore on a Sunday morning. I just didn't expect anyone else would be.

Somehow we all squeezed into a packed ferry that was one of those maritime throwbacks that can make you throw up. As the game old girl bounced across the waves, she evoked warm memories of white-knuckle rides to Batam. Those Batam speedsters always seemed to be skippered by Animal from *The Muppets*. I never ate breakfast before the ferry ride. There was always a risk of seeing it again before reaching Batam. The St John's Island ferry was less hazardous, but a lively jaunt nonetheless. Still, I spotted a gullible family gorging on a McDonalds breakfast. I greeted them later outside the St John's Island's toilets. The ferries are merciless little buggers.

Borrowing from a familiar storyline, St John's Island has found itself at a crossroads between old and new Singapore – a literal link now exists between its rustic past and its future economic potential. At a cost of some $300 million, a causeway has been built to join St John's Island to the previously unspoiled Lazarus Island, and sand has been imported from Indonesia (ah, the good old days) for an extensive land reclamation project joining Pulau Seringat with Lazarus and artificially knitting all three Southern Islands together. From the neighbouring Sentosa, water, electricity, gas and telecommunication have been brought over, making the islands potentially self-sufficient. Obviously, these expensive works were not carried out so the odd nature lover and amateur photographer could saunter over to snap sea cucumbers. There was talk of casinos, waterfront homes and an exclusive Mediterranean-styled resort modelled on Italy's Capri. But the idea was sensibly shelved in 2007. The hotels and casinos were eventually plonked elsewhere. Old Singapore was left alone, sort of, until 2013, when the Ministry of National Development announced that Pulau Seringat had been zoned for residential use under its Land Use Plan. A couple of decades from now, Singapore could be blessed with both Sentosa Cove and Pulau Seringat; two ghost towns for the rich toasting each other on opposite sides of the sea.

In truth, St John's Island doesn't scream "Capri" when you step off the jetty. It says former quarantine centre for cholera-stricken Chinese immigrants, quite literally, on the welcoming information board. The neglected island then held political detainees for a while before serving as a rehabilitation shelter for opium addicts. St John's Island is rarely confused for the Maldives.

But the isolation is its greatest draw card. My daughter loved the space and the opportunity to scoot along the water's edge with only the sea breeze and her vivid imagination for company. Much of my entire childhood was spent rummaging through overgrown green spaces and illegal tipping sites around my Dagenham housing estate, alone with my thoughts and a few glue-sniffers taking shelter in a burnt-out Ford Fiesta. It was such a liberating experience (as it was no doubt for the glue sniffers). There is something most satisfying about a child being unshackled in a wilder environment.

Accelerating away on her scooter, my little girl was in a happy, creative bubble until she stopped abruptly.

"Daddy, I think we should go back," she whispered over her shoulder. "There's a big man with birds staring at me."

At the end of a row of four shacks, presumably the remnants of an old kampong, there was indeed a hefty Chinese chap sitting on a deck chair, smiling through his sun-ravaged features. He ushered my daughter forward with a wrinkled, walnut-like hand.

"Come, come, see my birds," he said softly.

My daughter's apprehension was palpable. Even the kindly uncle picked up on it. I felt sorry for both of them. He was a sweet soul appreciative of some company. But my little girl lives on the mainland, where random strangers do not invite children into their home on the edge of a gloomy forest to admire their chickens.

"It's OK," I muttered. "Go and see the man with the birds."

"Yes, come and see, little girl," he said. "I've also got a mynah."

"A minor what?" I wondered aloud. "A boy or a girl?"

He never laughed either.

But he did have mynahs, chickens, roosters and other birds in cages and on the decaying roof of the wooden home. Around half a dozen unfriendly, feral and frankly disturbing cats patrolled the property with an air of genuine menace that suggested they'd previously eaten all other predators in the island's food chain. Omnipotent, they were the Komodo dragons of the cat world.

"Er, yeah, yeah, go and see the man's birds," I said, slowly stepping around a cat-like creature enjoying a snooze, presumably after eating one of the day-trippers.

While my daughter made cooing noises at the mynah, I realised that the fading huts all had furniture inside. "You live here?" I blurted out.

"When were you born?" he asked in reply.

"Er, 1974," I mumbled, distracted by a grey cat licking its scruffy paws with a tongue the size of a surfboard.

"Ah, you're a baby. I lived here since 1955."

"On St John's Island? I thought no one lived here any more."

"Only a few left. We work for Sentosa (Development Corporation). I help the boats come in, count the visitors, clean up a little bit."

He smiled as my daughter visibly relaxed around his beloved birds, poking her head up against the cage.

"You don't go back to the mainland?" I wondered.

"Twice a week for *makan*. I take the ferry," he pointed out, just in case I assumed he swam over. "Free one. I no need to pay."

"You think you will stay here?"

"Only the Government can decide."

"Do you want to go back?"

He examined my face intently for a moment, evidently taken aback by the question.

"What for? Over there got nothing for me."

He had parroted the taxi driver on the mainland. Both men held the same views on the other man's home. But my empathy belonged to the Bird Man of St John's Island.

WE CROSSED THE CAUSEWAY, taking in the spectacular views of the mainland on our left, the open sea on our right and the imposing, hilly forest of Lazarus Island ahead of us. Having spent more than 15 years poking my nose into Singapore's hidden bits, it's always exhilarating to step into unexplored territory for the first time. Most of all, I wanted to visit The Beach. I feel like the capital letters are earned because the isolated destination has developed a mythology online among backpackers and bloggers. There was The Beach of Lazarus Island. Not *a* beach, but *the* beach. Singapore has 63 islands, presumably all surrounded by sea and bordered with sand, some of it even natural, but they just had beaches. Lazarus Island had The Beach, the only beach worth visiting, a beach beyond the narrow imaginations of anyone raised on Sunday trips to East Coast Park. No matter what I read on Lazarus Island, everything came back to The Beach. There was nothing else like it apparently. The Beach defined New Singapore. It was alluring, exotic, micro-managed and almost entirely artificial. When the islands were joined through land reclamation, an area called Seringat-Kias was created with a beach bay carved into it like a knife slicing through an apple. The barges brought the sand, the ships brought the coconut plantation, a pond was fashioned just behind to collect rainwater to feed the trees (if nothing else, the foresight of Singapore's urban planners really should be commended) and the sexy island was suddenly curvy and shapely and ready for its luxury resort.

Only the resort wasn't built.

But The Beach remained, remote and slightly neglected, which added to its mystique. Reading about it online, the idyllic hideaway sounded like the work of Alex Garland and Danny Boyle. I feared an anti-climax unless this beach involved jumping off a 100m precipice into a rock pool before joining Leonardo DiCaprio in spearing sharks in a pellucid lagoon.

Naturally, we couldn't find it.

We followed the coastline along Lazarus Island and Pulau Seringat, trudging beneath the unforgiving sun and swishing away an invasion of some really angry wasps. But we found nothing attractive beyond a young Filipino couple holding hands under a hut. My exhausted, red-faced daughter and my exasperated wife dumped their bags on a bench in protest. The wasps hovered in the shelter's darkened alcove, like nightclub bouncers waiting to give us a kicking in the alley.

"That's it, we're stopping here," my wife declared in a huff, startling both the wasps and the Filipino couple on the opposite bench, who I suspect were settling down for a quick canoodle.

"What about The Beach?" I muttered softly.

"Sod the beach," she declared. "It's boiling hot, we've been walking for ages, your daughter's about to succumb to dehydration. We're on an island. We're surrounded by bloody beach."

"But it's The Beach," I pointed out.

"If you say that one more time, I'll hit you with her scooter."

"Daddy, I need to do a wee," the other lady in my life announced to everyone under the shelter.

The Filipino guy gave me a sorrowful nod. I'm sure he edged away from his partner. A bickering family is always an effective contraceptive device.

I grabbed my daughter's hand and ushered her towards some long grass to baptise Lazarus Island. Through the clearing, I saw a couple of guys in their early 20s fishing in a large pond. I lifted my daughter in the air, shook her thoroughly, sent her back to her simmering mother and set off towards the fishermen, eager for an excuse to slip away.

"Hey, man, I'm looking for The Beach," I called out.

He smiled knowingly.

"You passed it already, gotta go back, until you see a short path on your left with a shelter on the side, go through there. That's the beach."

Holding his rod with one hand and providing directions with the other, he spoke with an air of authority.

"How come you know so much about this place?"

"I work on St John's Island," said the affable Zaihan (not his real name, but this is Singapore).

"Yeah? What do you do here?"

"Take samples, check the water levels. Look for pollution. That sort of thing."

"Is the water clean?"

"No lah, it's sedimentation caused by land reclamation. We keep churning up all that sand, of course it will affect the water, even here."

"So that's changing Lazarus Island?"

He grinned at my ignorance.

"Everything's changing. You know when I first started working at St John's, used to see turtles and dolphins, pods of dolphins, almost every day, up by the causeway between the islands. Now only once in a while."

"Why?"

"Pleasure cruisers. When you get to the beach you will see. Even the *ulu* side of Singapore got to be for the rich now."

I grabbed the girls and followed Zaihan's instructions, swatting away the wasps along the path. My daughter spotted our Filipino friend in the long grass, fiddling with the button on his jeans.

"Daddy, what's he doing?" she asked.

"He's, er, bird-watching," I replied, dragging her scooter along.

"What kind of birds, Daddy?"

"Oh, er, cuckoo birds... Let's go."

We found The Beach.

At first, we wished we hadn't. We didn't want to go in. A shelter beside a sandy, litter-strewn path did indeed mark the entrance to the bay of Seringat-Kias. Polystyrene boxes and dumped bottles and cans were everywhere. Shards of glass and sharp, plastic pieces were partially, and cruelly, concealed by the sand, poking out just enough to tear through the soft flesh of a barefooted visitor. A black cat with a disturbing, bloodied face, the wounds still pulpy and fresh, devoured some bee hoon that had been left on a paper plate, content to share the noodles with hundreds of ants. An older couple occupied the shelter, picking away at the last of their picnic and leaving empty food packets and tin cans scattered across the stone floor, presumably working on the assumption that someone would clear their rubbish away at some point. Someone usually does.

While my wife took the scooter, I picked up my daughter and we tiptoed slowly through the man-made mess and over the wavy lines of flotsam and jetsam washed up on the shore to The Beach.

Well, the setting was just wonderful.

Artificial or not, the curved tranquil bay belonged in one of those tourism commercials where the Pan-Asian family run by in slow motion, all wearing billowing white shirts. It certainly didn't belong in Singapore.

Paddling in the sea with my daughter, I noticed something hairy and mammalian crawling along the sandy bottom, something I had never encountered before in the seas off Singapore: my own size 12 feet. The water was remarkably clear until it reached waist-height. The sedimentation process caused by the never-ending land reclamation had not quite reached the rear end of Lazarus Island. Floating on my back and watching the sunshine dazzle on the turquoise surface, I was drifting towards Old Singapore. This was *kampong* Singapore. Children splashed in the sea and made sandcastles on the beach with their parents. It was almost Raffles' Singapore, with the waves gently lapping against the sand and sliding towards the coastal forest. The Beach was peaceful and mostly unspoiled. Singapore still keeps a little paradise in its back pocket.

But they are coming.

With the predictability of the tides of the sea, they are coming. Lying on my back and staring up at the coconut trees swaying in the breeze offered an escape not only from the congested mainland, but also from the kings of the corporate jungle behind me. Zaihan was right. The wealthy had found their weekend retreat. Seventeen leisure cruisers of all grotesque shapes and sizes cluttered the lagoon, blocking the view, churning up the bay, increasing the noise and fuel pollution and scaring away any native marine life foolish enough to hang around. They didn't just visit Lazarus Island. They dropped anchors and planted flags. New Singapore's money had even filtered through to an obscure, quiet, offshore island, driven by the engines of yachts more expensive than most public housing on the mainland.

One potbellied expat, in particular, was testicles-tied-to-a-tree excruciating. Not content with a pleasure craft the size of a void deck hogging the middle of the bay, he insisted on whizzing around the lagoon in a petrol-powered dinghy, with its puttering, farting engine echoing across the beach. First, he dropped off some body-boards to a gaggle of obese kids submerged in the soggy sand at the water's edge. Then he returned from his yacht with some drinks. Then he made the round-trip again in his flatulent floating phallus to hand one of the kids some goggles. His yacht, just in case you were wondering, was moored no more than 25m off shore in calm, still waters. The temptation to invite the lazy fuckers to make their own way back to the yacht and kill two kilos with one swim was overwhelming.

There were no craggy-faced fishermen building *kelongs* off these vessels, just the usual trust fund babies and rich Asian and Western expats quaffing champagne and zig-zagging around on jet-skis. While my daughter and I played catch, I noticed a young Mainland Chinese couple sunbathing while a Malay lad cooked satay for them on the deck, drenched in sweat. I had seen a similar scene in a black and white documentary at the National Museum of Singapore, where subservient locals waited on wealthy foreigners. As I watched the expatriates toast themselves across the bay, I counted no Singaporeans on the yachts, beyond those cooking satay and no doubt swabbing the decks. Singapore's wealthiest residents can spend the money wherever they choose, but must they dominate everywhere? Marina Bay, Sentosa Cove, Shenton Way, the East Coast and most private housing estates (and a good few public ones) already fall within their purview. With Pulau Seringat zoned for residential use under the Land Use Plan, they'll end up owning those connected islands too. But the yachts and jet-skis are already here. Singapore's playground for the rich and shameless has been extended to include Lazurus Island.

Regular Singaporeans could be forgiven for thinking they are becoming those smokers at airports, herded into a small glassy room on the property's fringes and told to be grateful that they've at least got a room.

So I urge you to visit The Beach (the capital letters have been earned). Take a picnic (there are no food outlets) and plastic bags to bring the leftovers home again (there are hardly any dustbins). Make sandcastles with your kids. Make out with your partners (not in front of the kids). Enjoy the golden sand, the pristine beach and the swimmable sea while you still can. Old Singapore is on borrowed time here. The Southern Islands were joined for a reason. The invasion has already begun. Their yachts are moored in the bay. Just try not to think about them when you come to Lazarus Island. Ignore the gleaming status symbols cluttering the horizon line, like acne spoiling an otherwise flawless complexion.

The Bird Man of St John's Island doesn't have a care in the world, just lots of chickens and cats that could take down a buffalo.

The beach behind Lazarus Island is delightful, apart from the unexpected sea creatures. But the wealthy have got to have their beer parties somewhere.

Seven

I FOUND MYSELF playing Knock Down Ginger. For readers unfamiliar with the quirky English game, Knock Down Ginger does not involve striking anyone with red hair. It's a prank that dates back to the 19th Century and its name was lifted from a piece of British doggerel. Essentially, the game involves a gaggle of giggling mates tiptoeing towards a stranger's front door, banging on the door loudly and running off down the street before the residents answer. Admittedly, this game doesn't work so well in Singapore. The culprits would be found at the nearby lobby waiting for the lift. Even in England, I was a distinctly mediocre participant. I was saddled with the physique of a giraffe so I was spotted above garden fences and hedgerows. Plus I always seemed to knock on the door of the regional 100m sprint champion. I remember retiring after being pummelled into the pavement one drizzly evening.

In Chinatown's Neil Road, of all places, I came out of retirement for a final round. I was late for my date with a tour guide at Baba House. I had passed the magnificently restored Straits-Chinese terrace house before. Its distinct bluish-mauve façade was impossible to miss.

So of course, I missed it.

Perspiring heavily, I dashed along Neil Road, shouldering a heavy backpack before stopping outside the beautifully blue building. I slid the heavy bolt across, pushed open the iron gates, dashed across the courtyard of the private, prestigious property and rang the bell. The tour guide didn't answer. I rang the bell again and peered through the window and into the main living area. For a building that had been conserved and restored by teams of engineers, architects and master craftsmen from the National University of Singapore (NUS) and the Urban Redevelopment Authority (URA), the place was surprisingly post-modern in its minimalism. If anything, Baba House resembled a home office and study. Rather panicky, I banged the window with my fist. The tour had started five minutes ago. Finally, the penny dropped. There was no 19th Century period furniture. The interior was not draped in elegant Peranakan features. I was trespassing and thumping my fist against the window of what, by any conservative estimate, must have been a private property valued at around $10 million. When I heard a noise coming from the back rooms and spotted a shadow moving along a distant wall, I panicked. I inexplicably started running. I was a 40-year-old man playing Knock Down Ginger in Neil Road.

Further along the street, I stumbled through the gates of No. 157 Neil Road, the correct address, and dashed towards one of the most significant homes in Singapore.

In honour of her late father, Tun Tan Cheng Lock, Agnes Tan had made a donation of $4 million in 2005 to allow the university to purchase her Peranakan family home, restore its original features where possible and showcase a historic domestic culture in an appropriate setting. The URA-NUS conservation project exceeded all expectations. Tan Cheng Lock Baba House, to give the terrace home its full name, is one of those rare heritage stories with one happy ending after another. Everything went right. Everything looks and feels right about Baba House.

When I arrived, out of breath and a little worse for wear, the affable tour guide, Janice, invited me to put my rucksack in a cupboard to avoid knocking over any priceless vases. The NUS organises several tours of the house every week with a strict limit on numbers. The tours are free and usually filled quickly. My tour group was mostly expatriate women and a couple of American tourists, who said "gee, would you look at that flue" once in a while. Janice guided us into the courtyard to admire the elaborate façade of the three-storey property. The house was probably built in the 1890s, bought by the shipping tycoon Wee Bin around 1910 and, to achieve conformity, has been restored to how it looked in 1928. Above the second-storey windows were Chinese characters emphasising industry and prudence to reflect the occupants' virtues, rather like a family motto. I tried to recall if my childhood home had any similar mottos and thought of the one my mother hung in the bathroom: if you sprinkle when you tinkle, please be neat and wipe the seat. It wasn't Confucius, but no one peed on the carpet.

There were peony flowers and dragons beneath the windows, along with detailed Chinese fables that had been carved into stone. These wall coverings reflected the wealth of the homeowners, an architectural design quirk embraced by families everywhere. On my childhood housing estate in Dagenham, an original red-brick exterior suggested the residents still rented their homes from the council (conversely, a red-brick home in the countryside was a sure sign that the owner was posh). A pebble-dashed home was a quick attempt by the owner to show that the proud property no longer belonged to the council. And a home covered in stone cladding meant that the residents were marginally wealthier than the pebble-dashed people. My friend's parents were among the most affluent in the street and opted for something known as artexing in the UK, a then-fashionable surface coating that involved painting external walls in white, circular swishes. Whenever we passed the house, my mother always said: "He might be rich, but it looks like he's wiped his arse all over the wall."

No such critique could be levelled at Baba House.

The attention to detail could easily fill another book – and indeed will do so when NUS publishes one on the restoration project. The front living room was the swankiest because it was usually as far as visitors were allowed to venture. All business and hospitality was conducted there. The rest of the house was off limits to guests. This cultural tidbit delighted me. The Wees were wealthy shipping tycoons, with at least 16 homes in the area and 20 ships in what is now Keppel Harbour, but my mother shared their homely sensibilities. Whenever my granddad dropped us home, she would take me aside beforehand and say: "If he comes in, he's only going in the living room. The rest of the house is a shithole."

In the middle of Baba House was an airwell, seemingly at odds with the home's grand opulence. Despite the intricately carved doorways, golden picture frames and an ancestral altar that was bigger than the first room I rented in Singapore, the gaping square-shaped hole allowed rain to gush into the family room, essentially flooding the patterned tiles on the walls and floor. And yet, the water damage was slight. The guttering funnelled the rain into a specific catchment area, where the freshwater was once collected and stored for daily consumption. Considering Baba House has been exposed to an equatorial climate for more than a century, the airwell windows and walls were largely intact.

But it was the peephole that was the tour highlight. In the matriarchal bedroom, Janice pulled back a rug to reveal a small, rectangular piece of wood that had been cut out of the timber floor. She lifted the block to reveal a peephole into the front living room below. Old Grandma had literally kept an eye on the family shipping business, making sure the kids were making the right decisions with prospective clients downstairs. The elder generations had discreetly monitored their family's daily movements. That peephole was the Facebook of the early 20th Century. There was a second peephole closer to the front door, an ingenious device that allowed the residents to peer down at the hawkers and door-to-door traders without leaving the upstairs bedroom.

So you must visit Baba House. It's your history. Every piece of authentic furniture either comes from the Wee family – around 70 per cent – or was donated by Peranakan families in Singapore and Malacca, Malaysia. To my knowledge, Baba House is the only authentic showcase that accurately depicts how a Peranakan family lived, worked, entertained, ate, slept and spied on unsuspecting visitors in the 1920s. If you do not come for the cultural experience, at least come for the peephole.

NOW THE MAINLAND CHINESE are an easy target in New Singapore. Just about everything is their fault. Even if they are not involved, it is still their fault by osmosis. Recently, I shared a story on Facebook concerning an appallingly selfish family who had allowed their daughter to defecate in a potty at the Marina Bay Sands food court. Their fellow diners were appalled. I was no less shocked. I couldn't believe there was anyone eating at the Marina Bay Sands food court. Have you been to The Shoppes lately? There's more life at Bukit Brown Cemetery.

According to the news report, none of the outraged bystanders intervened to discreetly ask the mad family to airlift their crapping kid to the nearest public amenities. They performed that heroic act of civil disobedience in a brave new voyeuristic world. From a discreet distance, they whipped out their phone cameras with not a thought for their own safety. The citizen journalists filmed a semi-naked child doing a No. 2 and sent the video to the No. 1 online news site in town.

I only posted the story to make a facile comment about our increasing inability to publicly engage beyond posting or liking a cowardly video clip. But the comments on the newsfeed changed tack and the pooping family changed race. Somewhere along the thread, they became Mainland Chinese. The gist of the argument was that only the Mainland Chinese would treat their children like police horses, with a licence to shit in the street. When I tactfully pointed out that the story failed to disclose the family's race – and I'm not entirely sure the skin tone matters when a child is taking a shit in a food court – I also suggested that the grainy photos indicated a Caucasian family, rather than a Chinese one. Ah, but the Mainland Chinese did it first, came the lamentable reply.

That's the trouble with a generous immigration policy, apparently. Within minutes of those employment passes being laminated, foreign Chinese folks are lining up to drop their shorts in public places.

The stereotyping helps no one. However, there is an obvious visual drawback.

The Mainland Chinese have, generally speaking, perfected the admirable art, shall we say, of standing out in a crowd. As tourists, the Chinese are unique in their ability to make their presence felt on foreign soil, to assert their national pride, to broaden their cultural horizons by travelling the world and visiting every overseas Chinatown and TCM shop. Naturally, I stumbled upon a large China tour party in Chinatown outside a TCM shop. The cultural irony never ceases to amaze. I cannot begin to grasp the pointlessness of paying thousands of dollars to fly to, say, an

African country, only to be taken to Ye Olde London Town Tea Shoppe by a Cockney-speaking tour guide who's encouraging me to whip out the credit card because he's on commission for every box of lightly buttered scones I order.

After leaving Baba House, I enjoyed an aimless stroll around the Blair Plain conservation area. Gazetted for conservation by the URA in 1991, Blair Plain is a quiet community of two- and three-storey shophouses and terrace homes built from the 1880s. The cluster essentially incorporates the narrow streets of Blair Road, Spottiswoode Park Road and Everton Road and a handful of properties in Kampong Bahru Road and Neil Road, including Baba House. Blair Plain resonates not just for its history but for its eclectic range of styles. With New Singapore increasingly dominated by higher residential enclaves, Blair Plain is a step back to a freer, messier (and, yes, certainly richer) time for its residents. Chinese, Malay and European design elements have all been incorporated in the Art Deco and modern architecture (Everton Court is a favourite). Height is just about all the terrace houses have in common. No two homes look the same.

Walking among the wicker chairs, vintage lamps, stone lions and mosaic-tiled floors, I was struck by the silence. There was almost no traffic on the roads. But then I heard them before I saw them. The tour guide, carrying a Louis Vuitton satchel, was barking out tourism tidbits. As our paths finally crossed on Spottiswoode Park Road, their place of birth could not have been more immediately apparent if they had treated me to quick verse of *March of the Volunteers*. They communicated in a fashion that suggested they were hearing impaired. The group was almost entirely lost in a cloud of nicotine. And their matching attire suggested they had been wallpapered by Louis Vuitton.

They were so loud, so confident and so unapologetically self-assured that I found myself strangely drawn to them. I followed them into a TCM shop. The tour guide delivered his sales spiel and then dashed outside for a cigarette break. He hadn't had one for at least a minute. Once he left, it was a feeding frenzy. If the animal was endangered and dead and pickled and bottled and promised a wrinkle-free complexion, they wanted as much as their hand luggage could carry. Caught up in the stampede, I realised I had been handed a bottle of something medicinal to peruse by an attentive shop employee. I read the box. The brand was Shake Hand. It sounded like a sexual aid for those predisposed to having sex on their own.

The product itself was crocodile oil and, according to the box, was a terrific hand moisturiser. I couldn't help myself. I leaned across the counter.

"Excuse me, this crocodile oil, can go on the hand, is it?" I asked.

"Yah, this one for hand one," she replied.

I'm sure it was.

"But how did they know?"

"Eh?"

"How did they know that crocodile oil was a suitable hand moisturiser?"

I was desperate for her to reply: "Well, *ang moh*, there was this crocodile wrangler in the Northern Territory who once pulled a croc from the river and said, 'Shit, Mick, take a look at this, mate. I've been pulling that slippery bastard for an hour and I've got hands smoother than a baby's arse'."

But alas, she never really understood me and moved on to one of the tour party waving a platinum credit card across the counter.

Still, my new friends from the north proved to be a highlight of my wander around Blair Plain. I was reluctant to leave them, but they had to return to their tour bus and I was one breath away from needing a nicotine patch. They were brash, but entirely benign. In truth, they brought Blair Plain to life. If the peaceful walk around the conservation area was wonderful, the company was priceless. And I'll never forget the Shake Hand Brand.

A walk around Blair Plain is a walk around history, until the China tour parties turn up to buy crocodile oil.

*Baba House is one of Old Singapore's great heritage success stories.
Apparently, the Chinese characters do not say, "owe money, pay money".*

Eight

MRS BAVISTOCK was a lovely lady and a caring neighbour. But as a child, I thought she was a fruitcake. She lived in a rickety old cottage in our Dagenham street, practically an alien building among the red-bricked terraced houses of what was then the world's biggest public housing estate. She loved her cottage and was deeply proud of its Victorian heritage and was always eager to show it off.

Every time I delivered her free weekly newspaper, she'd open the door, hand me a couple of stale sweeties and say: "Hello, Neil, come in and see my cottage."

"No, I can't, I've got to deliver all the papers before it gets dark," I'd reply feebly.

"But the cottage is really, really old," she'd insist.

Yeah, so are you, you daft old bat.

I'm rather ashamed of the puerile thoughts of my prepubescent self now, but her timing was off. Around the time of her home invitations, I watched an episode of Roald Dahl's *Tales of the Unexpected* late one night, assuming it would be a jocular jape like *Charlie and the Chocolate Factory*, rather than the horrifying adults-only murder mystery it actually was every week. My particular episode was truly, truly terrifying. A large, chatty, elder woman in a headscarf, with more than a passing resemblance to my grandmother, invited a girl home to her neat, welcoming cottage to shelter from a passing storm. They giggled and skipped all the way home, where the woman's elderly husband sat at the kitchen table. He leered at the little girl in a sexually suggestive manner and the episode ended. I never saw Willy Wonka in the same light again. As I shivered in the darkness that sleepless night, I vowed to avoid both Roald Dahl and Mrs Bavistock for the rest of my life.

But she never gave up. The kind offer was always shouted over her rose bushes. There she stood, on the doorstep, in her house slippers and gesturing for me to explore her cottage, knowing that I had a keen interest in local history. But I was no fool. I knew there was a sex-crazed old man waiting for me at the kitchen table. Of course there wasn't, much to my relief (and perhaps Mrs Bavistock's disappointment. She spent far too much time playing with her geraniums).

More than 25 years later, I returned to my childhood street and was struck by how special Mrs Bavistock's home really was. The Halbutt cottages were once surrounded by Essex farmland. Most of them were demolished to make way for Dagenham's sprawling public housing estate, very much the Toa Payoh of London's interwar years. Inexplicably, a few were left standing, including Mrs Bavistock's home. They didn't fit the conventional narrative of their own environment. They were clearly out of place and out of time. They were just like Kampong Silat.

Wandering around the deserted housing estate off Silat Avenue, I kept thinking of Mrs Bavistock, proudly living in her outdated home. Like the Halbutt cottages, Kampong Silat had always trailed the world around it. The four blocks were built by the Singapore Investment Trust (SIT) between 1948 and 1952 and comprise the second oldest public housing estate in

Singapore (after Tiong Bahru). In some ways, they are four highly visible thorns in the side of the country's public housing story, often abbreviated as the HDB miracle. Every primary school child can recite the lines. The SIT's attempt at providing decent homes for Singaporeans was slow, insubstantial and unproductive so, in 1960, some smart HDB guys found a phone box, changed into their capes and saved the day. That's not to denigrate HDB's achievements in such a short period of time, but it does overlook a rather obvious prologue.

The Kampong Silat blocks are practical and quite elegant homes. Or at least they were until they were closed and the residents moved elsewhere in 2012. They were perfectly adequate then. They were spooky now. Even during the day, there is something troubling about an empty housing estate. The faded posters on the town council notice board, the discarded rice wine bottles on the grass, the boarded-up windows on the ground floor and the rusty, padlocked grilles across apartment doors and corridors gave Kampong Silat a disturbingly dystopian feel, part-apocalyptic sci-fi, part zombie horror. Homes should be occupied. When they are not, it's strangely unsettling.

Ominous thunderclaps didn't help and the gloomy clouds hovering above the red-tiled rooftops only added to the dream-like ambience. When the heavens inevitably opened, I took shelter beneath a covered walkway and admired the facing blocks. Only three or four stories high, the rectangular, turquoise buildings were adorned with the typically curvy Art Deco flourishes of the period. Their attractive window ledges and wall engravings were presumably too expensive for their practical HDB successors, but they were certainly prettier. Before land reclamation, this quirky village fronted the sea. To its credit, the URA gazetted the buildings in mid-2014. What the future is for such a unique housing estate isn't clear, but at least it has one.

And then, I saw the snake.

Kampong Silat was hardly a day trip to Disneyland before the reptile popped up. Billowing sheets of rain made their way across the deserted field and slapped my legs. The Art Deco shelter was pretty, but pretty useless as a shelter. I heard a rhythmic rattling noise drifting across the storm. It was coming from the corridor of the opposite block. Through the rain, I pictured Mrs Bavistock leaning up against the bars of the door grille and beckoning me towards her with a bony finger. I traced the sound to a rusting sign with a screw loose banging against the corridor wall in time with the storm's breeze. The sign read: "Keep Out, No Trespassing." Even Mother Nature had a macabre sense of humour. Drenched and all alone in a windswept, end-of-the-world ghost town, I made my way around the front of block 22 to at least be facing the populated Kampong Bahru Road. Hanging my rucksack on an old washing line suspended from the corridor's ceiling, I was wringing out my soaking clothes when, for reasons I still cannot fathom, I peered down at one of the small, square-shaped grates beside my foot. The grate cover was missing. The drain was exposed. Between a rusty, broken pipe and a floor filled with damp leaves, something black, long and slithery moved, just inches from my left foot.

Once, when I was about 10 years old, I had assumed I was dying. The topic was not up for discussion. I entertained no dissenting voices. I was bloody dying. Sitting in a pub garden, I had laughed and swallowed some lemonade at the same time. The drink went down what my mother calls "the wrong hole" and I began crying and choking at the same time before running to a railing fence and shaking its bars repeatedly like a chimpanzee in a zoo cage. Every so often, my voice returned to emit a high-pitched "ah". That's all it was, that's all my dying self could muster, a short feminine shriek of "ah", like a soprano sitting on a spike.

I never made that noise again, until I saw the snake.

Without moving or even twitching, I stood ramrod straight beside the open drain and released a quiet "ah". I couldn't move. My limbs had left me. In that moment, I discovered that the ingenious human body sends three signals; primitive, throbbing tribal beats that communicate danger. The first was the "ah". Retaining the imperious, upright posture of a drill sergeant, I stared at the distant traffic on Kampong Bahru Road and muttered: "Ah!… Ah!… Ah!"

The second, obvious signal was my heart thumping through the ribcage and the third was a faint, distant puffing sensation, like the gentle blowing of soft kisses. That was my sphincter. I was not in control of my bodily functions. There was an outside chance of me soiling myself.

In such perilous moments, I do not want to be Neil Humphreys. I want to be George McThickie (not his real name). George was in my class at school and was entirely oblivious to the world around him. While we worked on our French prepositions, he picked his nose. Whatever came from his nasal cavity was always greeted with wide-eyed wonder, as if the contents were entirely unexpected. Every day was one of happy discovery for George McThickie. I envied his blissful ignorance. He couldn't tell a snake from a garden hose. But I could. And I knew exactly what kind of snake it was.

Black spitting cobras do not appreciate being disturbed.

Their venom imposes clear relationship boundaries. If they spit in your eye, you go blind. If they bite, you die.

I took a half step backwards and the cobra craned its head, poking out that forked tongue to sniff the air. He knew I was within easy spitting distance. So did my sphincter. With each shuffling half step, I found myself making more noise than a buzzing chainsaw. The cobra froze, but didn't slither any closer.

The slow, backwards shuffle was easing the tension so I kept going, stepping and farting like a flatulent Michael Jackson doing the moonwalk (which worked really well with the occasional "ah" sounds).

Finally, my reptilian friend seemed satisfied that I posed no threat. As I finished my *Billie Jean* routine, he recoiled and disappeared beneath the fallen leaves. When I reached the bus stop on Kampong Bahru Road, I figured it was probably safe to stop running.

EAGER TO FORGET the snake, I headed down Kim Tian Road, turned right and entered a wonderful architectural enclave that epitomises the gentrification story in Singapore. It's a familiar tale with the same ending.

The prologue usually involves an eclectic bunch of urban planners and progressive thinkers who decide to drop a circus-shaped village of mostly red-brick homes and shops into the middle of a tropical Asian island. These groundbreaking buildings boast aesthetically impressive rounded balconies and spiral staircases that share design similarities with the housing estates of my East London childhood, but are nonetheless distinctly Asian. Initially, these homes are beyond the average blue-collar worker, but when the HDB housing boom explodes and affluence spreads to the second and third generations, old is out and new is in. Younger families head for the newer, utilitarian boxes in the mushrooming suburbs and leave the elderly to play with their bird-singing aviaries in that strange-looking, low-rise estate fraying around its circular edges.

But then, those utilitarian boxes swamp the nation. Suddenly, everywhere looks the same. It's all functional, formulaic and dull. There is an eagerness to look elsewhere to discover something – anything – different to the housing behemoths spreading across the island. New becomes stale and old becomes fresh. That impractical, ageing estate long ago left behind to Singapore's pioneers and their homemade tofu stalls takes on a certain irreverence and originality; an anarchic streak even. It goes against the architectural grain. It stands out in a crowd, a rebel with curves. The reclusive behaviour only adds to the appeal. So the old place becomes "hip".

And it's the beginning of the end.

Initially, the pioneering hipsters have their hearts in the right place. They add to the historic charm, rather than detract from it. They bring independent boutiques and unique bookshops selling illustrated children's books, increasing the foot trade overnight for long-established family businesses and hawker stalls. Tourists turn up to see what all the fuss is about in *CNN* features and travel blogs. Expats and locals alike are delighted to find an independent store that sells more than assessment textbooks and self-help comedies. And on weekends, nostalgic Singaporeans follow the heritage trails to show their disbelieving kids that they did once live in homes that didn't cause a neck-ache when you looked at the roof.

For a while, it's almost perfect, a brief glimpse of Rousseau's utopia, a comfortable, agreeable middle ground where landlords, retailers, residents, shoppers and day-trippers are all adequately rewarded and compensated for their environment's dramatic evolution.

And then, greed and snobbery take hold.

The landlords smell an extra dollar. The air-kissers discover unoccupied territory. Well-intentioned pioneers paved the way, but the wealthy will take it from here. The chance to plant a flag for air-flown Danish cheeses and hazelnut dacquoise becomes irresistible. Annexation is inevitable. Both old-timers and the pioneering hipsters look on with a mixture of bemusement and mild anxiety as the antique dealers and exorbitant restaurants muscle in like mobsters armed with lattes and Camembert. Rubbing their hands together, gleeful, myopic landlords embrace the new money, jacking up rents high enough to induce nosebleeds, high enough to price existing tenants out of their own community, high enough to scare away the farsighted folks who made the trendy quarter such an attractive proposition in the first place. And the hippest, swingiest joint in town falls victim to the very urban conformity it so gamely fought to break away from in the beginning.

Welcome to gentrification in Singapore. Welcome to Tiong Bahru.

There's no place quite like it. As I wandered around the streets of Kim Tian, Yong Siak and Moh Guan (all named after prominent Singapore-Chinese pioneers), I realised the architectural daftness of the place. Everything confuses the cynical eye. The curvy buildings favour red brick, but bear no resemblance to the boxy homes of my childhood housing estate (Dagenham was built just a decade before Tiong Bahru). Balconies and building edges have rounded corners and horseshoe shapes, but there are still long horizontal vertical lines. There are apartment blocks, but no taller than some of the multi-storey houses around the East Coast. And those spiral staircases and their perfect form are something else. Tiong Bahru's twisty, swirly, timeless staircases are Marilyn Monroe. The lifts of the modern apartment block are reality TV stars, very shiny, very forgettable. In so many ways, the size, shape, style and materials used in Tiong Bahru seem entirely at odds with one another. But it works. The estate was designed by the Singapore Investment Trust between 1936 and 1941 and yet – and this is the controversial bit – HDB struggles to match such architectural originality. Tiong Bahru is the most stylish public housing estate in Singapore.

But I was looking for its grubbiest part. I was looking for Tiong Bahru's historic bomb shelter because we all love a bomb shelter in Singapore.

When my mother first visited many years ago, she unpacked her suitcase and wondered where it could be stored in the cluttered apartment.

"Ah, just stick it in the bomb shelter," I said, with the air of indifference that comes after living in Singapore long enough to forget how absurd that sounds.

My mother stopped.

"You have a place to store bombs?"

"No, of course not. We have a shelter to protect us from bombs."

I yanked open the heavy metal door to the windowless, ventilated, reinforced concrete room. Like all responsible residents, our bomb shelter was suitably stocked for an emergency. We had some empty suitcases, an old mop and bucket, a box of Christmas decorations and mouldy tins of paints (should Singapore fall victim to a sustained bombing raid, I suspect most of its sheltering residents would succumb to paint fumes in a week).

"Why do you have a bomb shelter?" my mother asked, not unreasonably. "Are you at war with anyone?"

"Well, the neighbours' baby does keep screaming. But no, all apartments have bomb shelters," I pointed out, referring to the euphemistic "housing shelters" that have been incorporated into building designs since 1998.

My mother thought about the ingenious security measure for a moment.

"So what happens if your building gets bombed and collapses?" she said. "You're on the 20th floor."

"I don't know. We'll probably save the Christmas decorations."

To my immense regret, the graphically descriptive "bomb shelter" is slowly falling out of favour among (snobbier) Singaporeans. I visited a showflat recently and the real estate agent regurgitated the usual property jargon. She called the room a "storage area". Then it was a "potential walk-in closet". Then it was "an ideal location for your daughter's toys". And finally it was – and I'm not making this up – a "possible room for the maid if you want to use the utility room for something else". The room had no windows and the kind of impenetrable door usually found at the entrance of a Bond villain's volcanic lair. I had to ask.

"Why don't you call it a bomb shelter?"

The real estate agent fiddled with her welcome pack.

"Well, most Singaporeans prefer to use..."

"But it's a bomb shelter, right? A shelter from potential bombs, that's its essential design function. If the building goes down, my family and I are going to be left standing in our floating bomb shelter, on the 40th floor and waving Christmas decorations at passing helicopters."

Thankfully, Tiong Bahru's residents call a bomb shelter a bomb shelter and are justifiably proud of their heritage oddity. Of all the blocks on the estate, number 78 is the standout. Apart from being the tallest – locals once referred to the place as Tiong Bahru Gor Lau (five-storey flat in Tiong Bahru in Hokkien) – it was also the first public housing block to include a purpose-built air-raid shelter. In June 1939, a press report announced that a basement area in block 78 could be readily converted into a shelter and, when it wasn't protecting terrified residents from falling Japanese bombs, the room would double as a children's playground. There's an extreme interpretation of maximising a multi-purpose facility.

As always, I couldn't find it. Block 78 is so long and curvy, it is nicknamed the horseshoe block and straddles both Moh Guan Terrace and Guan Chuan Street. Wearily trudging around in the drizzle, I stopped an uncle in a skimpy white vest and flip-flops.

"Hey, uncle, I'm looking for this air-raid shelter!" I cried. "You know where ah?"

He gave me a blank look.

"Eh?"

"The air-raid shelter, very famous one," I continued.

"Famous what ah?"

Then I spotted a photo of the World War II air-raid shelter on a shophouse wall. "Ah that one ah. The air-raid shelter."

He peered at the poster. Suddenly, his eyes lit up. "Ah, bomb shelter. Come. Come."

He'd make a lousy real estate agent, but he was a damn fine Singaporean. He led me into the car park at the centre of the Tiong Bahru estate that offered a fascinating view of the backs of the Art Deco structures, revealing their rear entrances and those spiral staircases. He stopped in front of two locked, grey metal doors with slats for ventilation.

"Ah, there. Bomb shelter," he said, already walking away.

"Can I go inside?" I called after him.

"Cannot, always locked one."

His voice trailed away.

With the air-raid shelter locked, I read the excellent information panels and learned that the place was used, but infrequently. Despite the populated Tiong Bahru area, it wasn't a primary target. The Japanese bombers were after the nearby Singapore General Hospital. The bomb shelter was later used by HDB as a "storage space" (oh, the irony), before the Singapore Heritage Board opened up the place for public tours in 2012 to mark the 70th anniversary of the country's fall to Japan. Quite rightly, the old place wasn't cleaned up or made too safe and sanitised.

After peering through the slats, I noticed the bolt and padlock. They had somehow missed each other. The doors hadn't been locked properly. Overwhelmed by a hot flush of mild anarchy, I slid the bolt across and pulled. The door creaked. I took a couple of tentative steps inside the murky basement and thought of my late grandmother. She spent much of The Blitz in an air-raid shelter, huddled together with her family on London Underground station platforms. To her, those shelters were spirited, communal places with a convivial atmosphere, full of carousing Cockneys filling the dank air with uplifting songs about Hitler only having one testicle. She spoke of warm-hearted communities united in both their hardship and defiance. I tried really hard to picture my Nan singing *Hitler Has Only Got One Ball* because I was appalled by my unease. An empty World War II air-raid shelter is a lonely, unsettling place, even during the day.

I heard a distant echo in the basement and ran back into the street.

"Come on, Neil, get a grip," I said aloud to no one. "You're a grown man. Get back in there."

Venturing into the damp cavern a second time, I used the light on my phone as a guide. The corridor was long and narrow and bordered by two brick walls. Rusty, exposed pipes left mouldy streaks along the walls and concrete. A solitary sign offered a reminder that I was still in literal Singapore. It read: "Air-Raid Shelter." That was a relief. I thought I had stumbled into a penthouse showflat. I kept going, but my thumping heart really wasn't in it. There was the trespassing. But there was also the cowardice. Darkness gets scarier when it gets darker. It didn't make sense to me either. But the absence of light, the steady tapping against leaky pipes and my loneliness all conspired against me. I had seen enough, which was almost nothing.

And yet, I felt exhilarated. I had found and touched a piece of Old Singapore, authentic and still in working order. The shelter survives, ironically, because it was rarely used. But Tiong Bahru families did huddle there in the weeks after Japan's bombing campaign began in 1941. The air-raid shelter was a remarkably well-preserved Singaporean artifact with few alterations and I had explored a bit of it without official permission. My grandmother would have approved.

That should have been the end of my Tiong Bahru tour.

I had skipped along the happy side of gentrification. The Art Deco curves, the restored apartments and the excellent bookshops, the heritage signposts and trails, the hidden bomb shelter and my local tour guide had all suggested a successful meshing of old world and new; a clear attempt to work with the established community rather than suffocate it beneath Prada cushion covers.

But in my search for a bus stop, I stumbled upon Eng Hoon Street. An antique shop displayed prices that made the eyes water. A sign proudly informed any misguided peasants that this particular cesspool of ostentatious wealth was "by appointment only". These folks luxuriated in their elitism, literally pinning their badge of honour to the door. The street had the usual international bars, restaurants and children's boutiques selling half a dozen items on padded hangers. Singaporeans had mostly vanished, replaced by expat housewives power-walking past me in lime green Lycra. (I'm just putting this out there, but the whole expat Lycra thing – is it a law? Does the Lycra suit come with the expat package? Or does the Ministry of Manpower give away a year's supply of spandex and a free yoga mat with every dependent's pass?)

I stopped outside a cosmetic shop to gawp at the surreal scene being played out on the other side of the window. A woman sat back in a chair, chatting animatedly on the phone, her hand covered in more rings than a Peter Jackson trilogy. She held out her other hand for a shop lackey to work furiously around the cuticles, polishing and buffering as if attending to an old Volkswagen. Another shop employee kneeled at the woman's bare feet, trimming and pruning and treating the painted toenails like a garden hedge. I was again taken back to that smug documentary I had watched days earlier at the National Museum of Singapore, where locals waited on their colonial masters hand and foot. The scene was playing out in front of me. I heard a plummy narrator saying: "And in Tiong Bahru, there is no need to queue among the common folk as shop visits are by appointment only. You are free to peruse that essential $10,000 coffee table, safe in the knowledge that uninvited poor people will not disturb your shopping. Meanwhile, there are always a couple of natives on hand to remove that troublesome bum fluff from the crevices of your toes."

The buffed woman in the chair yawned. She had obviously had a hard day.

As I left the exhausted woman to her primping, I wondered if Eng Hoon Street foreshadowed Tiong Bahru's future. The estate's buildings are mostly protected but who ends up occupying them is anyone's guess. If landlords continue to impose unrealistic rent demands on tenants, then Tiong Bahru will be overrun by fawning pedicurists, Parisian menus and appointment-only antique dealers. They all have a target audience. But I'd rather spend the day locked in the air-raid shelter. At least it's local.

Boarded up but preserved, Kampong Silat has an uncertain future. But it's onto a winner with its snake laxatives.

Curvy, classy and elegant, Tiong Bahru is in a league of its own, as long as it doesn't suffer death by cappuccino.

Tiong Bahru's air-raid shelter is long, dark and smelly. I can't be any more descriptive because I got scared and left.

Nine

SENTOSA is in a state of permanent makeover. The island is an ageing Hollywood actor with trout lips, a wrinkle-free forehead and a face that last moved in 1975. It's forever being squeezed, stretched and injected with tourism implants to hold off the ageing process. It's like spending a day with Cher. Sentosa is never finished, never left alone. The name means "peace and tranquility", but the place is rarely allowed to enjoy either. Sentosa seems like it's one makeover away from turning into a horrifying, scarred, artificial mask of its former self, like Barry Manilow singing about Copacabana showgirls without moving his lips.

I stepped off the shuttle bus at Siloso Point and was confronted with not one but two colossal building sites. I had picked the western corner of the island to visit its remnants of Old Singapore and found myself peering up at the clanking construction of another money-spinner. I knew one site was for a new cable car station. I had no idea about the other.

"Excuse me, what's that?" I asked a passing Sentosa employee, pointing towards the steel girders rising above what was left of the island's lush forest.

"That's gonna be the new Sky Walk," the young guy said cheerily. "Haven't finished yet."

"No, I can see that. But it looks so high."

"Ya lah," he beamed. "Visitors can walk right above the forest across Siloso."

I craned my head to take in the steel walkway's extraordinary height. "So they've cut down the forest, to build a bridge for people to look at the forest?"

"Yeah."

"How will they get up there?"

"They can take a lift," he said, before turning serious. "But haven't finished yet."

"No, again, I can see that. The 'Keep Out' signs and the incomplete bridge suggested that."

I made my way to the Fort Siloso tram and joined a Malaysian family waiting for the driver to take us to Singapore's only restored coastal gun battery. We did that respectful nod at each other as I boarded the tram and ignored the slightly uncomfortable silence until I decided to pipe up.

"What made you decide to visit Fort Siloso?" I asked.

The husband gestured towards his wife and three children and replied: "It's cheap. Sentosa so expensive now."

But the island's increasing costliness hasn't scared visitors away. Sentosa keeps on building and they keep on coming. More than 19 million people visit the island each year, but few appear to make the trip to Fort Siloso (there are no blackjack tables for a start). The Malaysian family was dropped off to play a laser tag shooting game first so I alighted at Fort Siloso Square alone. The old military base was eerily quiet. I was the only one there. Feeling sorry for me, the young tour guide acted as a brief chaperone around the square, underlining the fort's highlights.

"Those guns over there are replicas," he began. "And you'll find more replica guns over there. Also, we have the Surrender Chambers, showing the exact set-up of when the British surrendered to the Japanese and then later when the Japanese surrendered to the British."

"Didn't the British surrender at the old Ford Factory and the Japanese at City Hall?" I enquired.

"Wah, you know your history ah. Which country you from?"

"Bedok."

"And you come to Fort Siloso?"

He wasn't making the greatest sales pitch for his tourist attraction. But I appreciated his time – and his company – and politely waited for him to complete his spiel.

"So if I've got this right. Most of the guns are replicas and they came from elsewhere. Both of the World War II surrenders happened elsewhere. The British army herb garden is artificial and some of the area is now devoted to a laser quest shooting game, where teenage kids run around with glowing guns and chest plates looking like the cast of *Cats*. Is that right?"

"Pretty much."

But the history is real. It's easy to be facetious, but Fort Siloso is a fabulous place, mostly because it stinks. The fort was built in 1874 and the gun batteries established in the 1880s, which was perhaps the last time the tunnels were cleaned. Aside from a coat of whitewash and some fans, the old barracks have been remarkably well preserved (i.e. neglected). A unique aroma of rusting metal and damp walls and floors permeates the whole place. While I watched the first of three videos in a darkish, chilly underground room, it hung in the air. I hadn't encountered the smell since I visited my great-grandmother as a child. I think it was left over from World War II.

In the corridors of underground batteries and gun-loading areas, waxwork figures depicting the British army stood in puddles of stagnant water. Green mould ran down the walls and rusting ammunition hoists gave a real sense of authenticity.

Speakers provided sound effects of cannons being fired and officers barking orders. Air-raid sirens, screaming Singaporeans and the marching boots of the invading Japanese army were heard in corridors so dark, I had to feel my way along the damp, cold walls. The sound effects were hardly subtle, but the unusual experience was a long way from casinos and endless coach parties following a flag-waving man to a cheap buffet lunch.

The atmospheric mood was far less terrifying than the spelling, though. On one marvellously incompetent information panel, I was reliably informed that "the Fort Serapong are is now the Sentosa Golf Club". The "are is" was how the sentence was written. The sign also pointed out that many of the pre-war buildings on Sentosa were used for "millitay purposes".

Shortly before I visited Fort Siloso, Singapore's sign-writing and grammatically gonzo information panels and public banners had caused a bit of a national embarrassment. A constituency banner in Mountbatten invited all its residents to have a "Marry Christmas" and a road sign was translated wrongly in Tamil. The emphasis on bilingualism in the last decade or so has achieved wondrous things in Singaporean society. Written and spoken English have both declined with alarming haste. Mandarin might have improved (even if many locals and Mainland Chinese continue to insist otherwise), but so many Singaporeans have been left with a bit of a chip on the shoulder and an inferiority complex over their linguistic inadequacy in two languages rather than one. The only dialect that unites almost everyone on the island, and is delivered with confidence, flair and screw-you panache, is still frowned upon in some snobbish circles and shunned like a form of linguistic leprosy. Singlish may not be to everyone's taste, but it's a vast improvement on "millitay purposes" and "Marry Christmas". At least Singlish makes sense.

Oh, Fort Siloso's overseers might also wish to reconsider their information panel outside the Surrender Chambers. With much gravitas and heavy bold fonts, a line read: "The worst disaster in British military history – M.W. Churchill, British Prime Minister, 1940-1955." The late Clement Attlee might query the attribution, considering he was British Prime Minister from 1945-1951 and ushered in the National Health Service, one of the most groundbreaking social welfare reforms of the 20th Century.

But the Surrender Chambers was a fascinating exhibit. A waxwork tableau recreated the historic surrenders of both the British in 1942 and the Japanese in 1945. The Japanese surrender was particularly impressive with accompanying TV footage of the City Hall event, but the British surrender was bizarre. The figures all looked the same. Now I know Lieutenant-General Arthur Percival and his subordinates didn't fare particularly well in the Fall of Singapore and history hasn't been kind to them, but neither were their waxwork sculptors. The three men sitting on either side of Percival at the table seemed to share his features – four balding, mousey-haired *ang mohs* with moustaches and farcically large noses. I wanted to find my Fort Siloso tour guide and ask if Caucasians really do all look the same to Asians. And had the British military high brass in Singapore been afflicted by alopecia? Perhaps the officers had taken hair from the receding pate and stuck it on the top lip to distract from that enormous conk. Either way, four white men all looking comically similar and sitting side by side made for a disconcerting spectacle. The Japanese must have thought they were conquering the Marx brothers.

Still, Fort Siloso was a wonderfully weird way to spend a couple of hours in a quiet corner of Sentosa. The World War II museum's incongruity and isolation remains its biggest selling points. Whether gun batteries and smelly military exhibits sell enough tickets to preserve the place is a question easily answered by the towering behemoth already overshadowing the cannons and gun complexes. The new cable car station and Sky Walk will increase the foot traffic, raise expectations and demand an inevitable attraction makeover. If I were you, I'd see Fort Siloso before it's turned into Asia's first light and laser interactive re-enactment of the Fall of Singapore with dancing fountains.

For the time being at least, Fort Siloso provides a brief respite from all that organised fun and gaiety. It's also an attraction with an endorsed, positive conclusion. When I left the Surrender Chambers, there was a potted history after 1945 displayed on the wall. Not surprisingly, the rousing chronology culminated with the 1959 General Election victory of the People's Action Party. Every Singapore story needs a happy ending.

LIKE MANY PEOPLE, I can pinpoint the turning point in my relationship with hospitals. At the risk of sounding trite, hospitals reflect life. Or at least they have in my case. As a child, trips to hospitals were little injections of youthful vitality. Those long, orderly corridors were bursting with colour. Every occasion was a kaleidoscope of newborn siblings and cousins, beaming dads and exhausted mothers and older relatives spoiling me at the hospital gift shop. There was the odd visit for stitches or a tetanus injection, but a lollipop eased the discomfort. Death didn't really happen in hospitals. If it did, I was mostly shielded from it. Death happened to other people, older people. Death had nothing to do with me in hospitals. Hospitals were a laugh. They were the world's cleanest children's playgrounds.

And then I got the first of many ingrowing toenails not long before I left for Singapore. As I sat on a hospital examination bed, medical interns surrounded my foot. These young people were around my age. They stared at my revolting big toenail, pulling faces to emphasise how disgusting it was while the resident doctor jabbed it with a pointy stick and said: "Yes, this one is particularly ugly, isn't it? You see how it's turning green in the corner and curling in at the sides like a pair of ram's horns? Sometimes it's called a ram's toe. Normally, we don't see such a physically unattractive condition on someone so young, but hey ho."

The novelty of visiting hospitals wore off shortly after.

As I made my way through the elegant gardens of Alexandra Hospital, I thought about how our relationships with hospitals change. I thought about my grandmother. She often regaled visiting relatives with her World War II stories and I once told her about the Alexandra Hospital Massacre of February 1942.

"Shame," she said. "But that's what they were like then, them Germans."

I never had the heart to correct her, partly because she was a difficult woman to interrupt, but mostly because she had no real idea where Japan was. But she loved the Second World War. She understood the atrocities and the inconvenience of the Germans dropping bombs on her childhood home and destroying her framed swimming safety certificate. (She never, ever forgave the Germans for that. As she always pointed out: "I dived down and got the brick, Neil. Me mother put the certificate up and it was lost when the Germans bombed us out, the bastards.") But she missed the camaraderie and the sense of personal and collective sacrifice. Strangers never bought her a gin and tonic in peacetime (I don't think she ever forgave the Germans for that either). The last time I visited a British hospital was to see my grandmother. She was sleeping and probably didn't know I was there. So I whispered some of her favourite war stories to her and held her hand.

She died in early 2014.

I abhor hospitals now. The innocence is gone. Death and hospitals are no longer abstract concepts that belong to other people. Thankfully, and beautifully, the folks at Alexandra Hospital, the URA and among the local Queenstown community understand that. There's no need to recall the ghastly atrocities of the Alexandra Hospital Massacre again. Any Google search – and my previous books – will do that. Preserving the building, honouring the lives lost in a dignified manner and recognising the pivotal role the hospital played in nurturing a fledgling Singaporean community are all that matter now. And every box has been ticked. In June 2014, Alexandra Hospital was added to the list of gazetted conservation buildings; another small, but not insignificant, pocket of Old Singapore spared. The neoclassical building peeks out through the dense foliage and is a fine example of practical, but tasteful, military architecture of the 1930s.

Really, it's a hospital in a garden. In a lush, green valley between the hospital buildings and Alexandra Road sits a rolling, landscaped garden with 500 plant species. Under the canny direction of the hospital's chief gardener and eco-warrior Rosalind Tan, a butterfly trail has been designed around nectaring plants. There were butterflies everywhere when I visited. And the garden was filled with dozens of those alien objects rarely found in shopping malls: benches. Near the top of the valley beside a fountain, I found a blue commemorative plaque honouring the soldiers and staff killed in the massacre. It wasn't glorified or melodramatic (I've visited American World War II memorials so over the top in their presentation, it's a wonder actors aren't employed to re-enact the combat brutality to the tune of the *Star Spangled Banner*). The tribute was simple and sincere and deeply affecting. War and death once marched towards Alexandra Hospital; now the site was peaceful, reflective and teeming with life. Singapore's splendid "hospital in a garden" was just about perfect.

As I took a final stroll around the butterfly trail, I thought again about my own World War II hero. My grandmother also had a glorious garden and I once asked how she managed to maintain all those rose bushes, the apple tree and the manicured lawn.

"Ah, that was your granddad," she replied, smiling at the memory. "He was always fucking about with his garden gnomes."

British soldiers keep watch at Fort Siloso. They are looking in the wrong direction for the Japanese, so it's an accurate reconstruction.

A hospital in a garden, Alexandra Hospital makes for such a poignant World War II memorial and heritage site.

Ten

MY SISTER will never forget her first visit to Singapore. Just a couple of hours after landing at Changi Airport, she dragged her jetlagged body to the crowded Queenstown Stadium. And then she saw her big brother. I was at the back of the concrete terrace, an obvious white face rising above the singing, swaying throng of local supporters. On my immediate left was a group of young Malay lads and girls, faces painted in red and white and waving pom-poms. Their choreography was simple but uncoordinated, thanks largely to a randy little sod who kept trying to hug the pretty dancing girls like a confused, excitable puppy trying to hump a chair leg. On my right was a large Chinese guy, possibly in his late teens or early 20s, who thrashed away at his large drum. His work ethic was exemplary. He only drummed when the ball was in play. And in the middle of this colourful maelstrom stood an *ang moh* who'd been in the country less than a year and yet, extraordinarily looking back, found himself leading the wonderfully diverse Tanjong Pagar United Fan Club. Between the drummer, the pom-pom performers and the horny 10-year-old trying to grab anything female, my job was to rouse the crowd by leading the chorus of "de-fend, clear the ball… de-fend, clear the ball… de-fend, clear the ball".

It took me a week to learn the lyrics.

Oh, and I had a megaphone, just in case I couldn't quite be heard in Johor.

This was my sister's first glimpse of her brother in his new country, surrounded by locals of all ages, a collection of Queenstown kids, a deranged drummer and a 10-year-old jumping on the prettiest pom-pom girl. I remain unapologetically proud of that surreal first encounter between siblings. Rather than the clichéd Raffles Hotel and the Padang, her introduction to Singapore was an authentically fruity slice of local life (which was propitious as I could afford neither Raffles Hotel or the Padang at the time). It's also a time capsule now. Such a warmly weird welcome to the tropical island is no longer possible at the same location.

With ironic timing, Tanjong Pagar United have been asked to sit out the struggling S-League. That cultural connection between the community and its local sports complex has been severed, temporarily at least (the Jaguars may return if the S-League experiences a sudden injection of capital to financially sustain more teams in Singapore's only professional football league. It's an interesting theory and certainly more plausible than, say, snow falling on Queenstown Stadium). What's sadder perhaps is the historical context.

The Queenstown Sport Complex happens to be the nation's first neighbourhood sports complex. Opened in 1970 to considerable fanfare, the stadium boasted a football pitch, a running track, elevated seating for 3,000 and five swimming pools. Considering much of Queenstown was still jungle in 1970 – and still is around Margaret Drive and Kay Siang Road – the pioneering sports hub must have made quite an impression (if I use the word "hub" again, you have my permission to shoot me. I was seeking an alternative to the overused "complex" and "stadium". I promise not to do it again). The place was also used for the National Day Parades in the 1970s and 1980s, a fact I learned from the excellent information panel outside the stadium. Quite rightly, the sports complex is part of the Queenstown Heritage Trail.

But the old photographs of families flocking to the pools contrasted sharply with the drab, rusting stadium that greeted me on a Saturday afternoon. Under a peeling sign that read "Jaguars, established 1975", a pitiful window display showcased Tanjong Pagar jerseys from the S-League era. Three guys jogged around the track. An overdressed uncle trudged slowly around the bitumen with a slightly puzzled look that suggested he'd taken a wrong turn and couldn't find the coffee shop. Feeling sentimental, I sat on the same concrete block where I once screamed, "de-fend, clear the ball" to impress my visiting sister. The stadium was a dusty, neglected shell of a once vibrant community attraction, drawing only nesting pigeons to its gallery. Sports clubs should bring local people together. Shortly before revisiting Queenstown Stadium, my brother had told me that the two sports centres of my Dagenham childhood had made way for housing. They were the only social outlets we had beyond the local park and the church youth club, where my only contribution to the weekly religious discussions always seemed to be, "yes, Nigel, the animals went in two by two... can we play table tennis now?"

Queenstown cannot go the same way.

My sister loved her first night in Singapore at the country's first neighbourhood sports complex. Everyone in the crowd treated her like one of their own, offering her curry puffs and prawn crackers. She joined in with the chanting (once she had learned "de-fend, clear the ball" and "referee *kayu*", she had pretty much exhausted our repertoire). Tanjong Pagar won the game and I kept her well away from the randy, humping kid. She still has fond memories of Queenstown Stadium along with tens of thousands of Singaporeans. Like Tanjong Pagar United, the old place deserves a comeback.

OK, NOW FOR THE REALLY UGLY BIT. Queenstown and Dagenham have far more in common than I had anticipated. They were first. They were pioneers of public housing. Other public housing projects preceded them in both Singapore and England, but their sheer scale was unprecedented, representing a concerted, centralised effort to build a town with decent educational, health and entertainment amenities. But there is always a price to pay for being first in public housing. Facilities falter. Homes decay. Reputations fall even faster. What was once a badge of honour can become a social stigma.

In other words, being from Dagenham is both sublime and shit.

The independence, resilience and street smarts instilled by a roughish childhood growing up in a mildly deprived household are priceless qualities in adulthood. But these qualities are negated somewhat by the condescension. Even in expat and writers festival circles in Singapore today, the mere mention of "Dagenham" can trigger smug comments between cappuccino sips. Sometimes the working-class background affords bragging rights. Sometimes it's a ball and chain.

With the increasing rich and poor divide in New Singapore, heartland kids get a similarly raw deal (even the "heartland" tag has a patronising whiff about it, a demeaning label passed down from on high). I know these kids. I meet them at neighbourhood school talks all year round. Sharp as tacks and so often wittier than the most scholarly of government scholars, they are punished by their postcode, pigeon-holed by a society that insists on putting every individual in a box. We label races, genders, sexualities, nationalities, ages and intellects and even make a point of distinguishing rich cosmopolitan folks from poor heartlanders. From Primary 1 placements and their catchment areas, kids are stamped from the moment they pick up a pencil in kindergarten. Some are screwed before they really get started, making a mockery of the whole meritocracy thing.

If you remain sceptical, come and visit Singapore's first HDB flats.

I had expected, and hoped, to record something else entirely. The first HDB flats provide a physical testament to a seismic shift in the country's socio-economic evolution, the moment when the baton for public housing was passed from distant colonial masters to committed local leaders. When the British-established Singapore Investment Trust was dissolved in 1959, three seven-storey blocks in Stirling Road were only half completed. HDB finished the job. In an unassuming, surprisingly tranquil street, those first HDB blocks still stand.

But there was no blue plaque, no Queenstown Heritage Trail sign and no photo gallery, nothing to commemorate the achievement. I'd like to think the apparent oversight was a deliberate attempt to respect the residents' privacy.

I'd like to think that.

But Singapore's first HDB blocks are not fit for celebration. They are not fit for habitation, unless the apartments are radically renovated. A spray-painted mural on the side of each of the three blocks was by far the most aesthetically appealing aspect of the dilapidated buildings. I took the staircase of the nearest block and climbed the seven storeys with my t-shirt covering my nose. A fetid stench hung in the stairwell, leaving me nauseous. My eyes watered. On the fifth floor, I leaned on the handrail and retched. The smell was an uncomfortable mix of stale tobacco, rotting food and rusting metal. The stairwell walls were patchy and peeling and spattered with chilli streaks. Armies of ants attacked rancid chicken bones and durian husks. Bags of rubbish occupied almost every floor and the floors themselves were covered in a carpet of cigarette butts. The only positive feature was the view on the seventh floor, taking in the sports stadium and swimming pools below.

Lee Kuan Yew had always championed Singapore's aggressive home-ownership policy, often recalling his trips to the UK and how shocked he was by the systemic neglect of rented properties. He wasn't wrong. I still recall long summer evenings spent in my sister's bedroom, attacking her rotting window frame with a screwdriver so the council would replace it. They refused. So both my sister and I went to work with the screwdrivers. The council relented. My sister got a new bedroom window. That was life growing up in an ageing property rented from the council. My upbringing was little different to the families living in the first HDB blocks. Being so old and starved of the basic amenities that newer estates take for granted, the three Queenstown blocks are now home to mainly rental residents. They are part of the other, less palatable statistic.

Singapore's home-ownership rate hovers around a remarkable 90 per cent, one of the highest in the world, a statistic worth bragging about (and, believe me, an opportunity is rarely missed in the media). The residents of the nation's first HDB blocks mostly make up the other 10 per cent, just as I did growing up. From the National Museum of Singapore to every local school and regional library, the HDB success story is parroted with such drum-banging frequency that I naively expected its prologue to be documented and celebrated. But its birthplace is neglected and, to all intents and purposes, ignored, rather like its residents. Rented or otherwise, HDB can surely do so much better than this.

It's easy to romanticise Singapore's first HDB village. It's easy to see something that isn't really there. From the other side of Stirling Road, I watched a toddler, naked but for a grubby diaper, playing in front of her family's ground-floor unit. She waddled among the rusting washing stands, the plant pots and the piles of junk dumped along the common walkway. With no playgrounds, shelters, gardens or even a void deck, she was left to her own devices. Some might see an adventurous child, revelling in the space and freedom once permitted in the kampongs of Old Singapore but denied in the homogenous housing estates of New Singapore. But I just saw a forgotten kid with no options beyond running around a tiny piece of cracked concrete covered in cat shit.

She deserved better, as do all of the residents of Stirling Road. The first HDB blocks represent a period in history no less relevant than the opulent Baba House in Neil Road. But unless the buildings and their occupants are afforded the dignity they deserve, this piece of Old Singapore will not be worth saving.

WHEN I left Singapore's first HDB flats, I needed cheering up. You probably do, too. So let's talk about something completely different. Let's talk about gay penguins.

Sometime in June 2014, I was sitting in a hotel room and staring at the planes landing at Rio de Janeiro Airport feeling isolated and lonely. I had been dispatched to Brazil to cover the World Cup, which was fabulous, but found myself in an airport hotel that could only have been further from Copacabana Beach if it was in Kallang. The phone rang. I answered slowly, expecting a request for another story with a time-bending deadline.

"Neil, a children's illustrated book on penguins has been banned."

I wasn't expecting that. It was my wife. We were under explicit instructions to call each other only in an emergency. The cost of calling Singapore from my Rio hotel room could be absorbed, but only by selling my vital organs.

"What are you talking about?"

"Someone on Facebook has said that Singapore has banned a children's book on penguins."

A bead of sweat trickled through my hair and down the back of my neck. My hands were suddenly clammy. Thoughts of Ronaldo and Messi were replaced by images of *Abbie Rose and the Magic Suitcase*. That's the name of my children's book series. And that's not a shameless plug. That's the name of paralysing fear. At that time, the latest *Magic Suitcase* story involved penguins.

"Is it my book?" I squeaked down the phone. "It can't be my book, right?"

"I don't think so," said my wife, before taking the conversation to a higher, psychedelic plane.

"This story is about gay penguins."

"That's very funny. Do you have any idea how much this call is costing us?"

"No, I'm serious. A library has banned a children's book because it's got gay penguins."

I picked up the tension in her voice. She was not joking. But I was still struggling. The adjectival "gay penguin" has a certain oxymoronic quality about it. It's not that penguins cannot be gay – of course they can – I just found it difficult to picture anyone who might care. An individual who actively combined oxygen and the cognitive process to express an opinion on the gender of fictional penguins in a children's illustrated book had to belong in an old Benny Hill sketch. Real people did not concern themselves with the behaviour of gay penguins, surely.

"But what does a gay penguin even look like?" I sputtered down the phone. "How do you illustrate a gay penguin? Does it listen to Judy Garland records? Does it wear a Native American headdress and sing *YMCA*?"

In a state of panic, I opened a PDF version of my penguin book and searched for any images that might be misconstrued. I found none because I had no idea what I was looking for. I clicked on the Google search bar and, for possibly the first and only time in my life, typed in the words "gay penguins", desperately hoping I wouldn't be directed towards the kind of animal porn website that causes a red light to start blinking in a CIA field office.

My screen exploded. Penguin-gate had rocked our little island. Singapore had been invaded by the march of gay penguins. Of course, it wasn't my book. Following a handful of complaints, the National Library Board (NLB) declared its intention to pulp all copies of *And Tango Makes Three*, an American children's story about two male penguins raising a baby chick in Central Park Zoo. The content was deemed to be against the city-state's family values. I moved to Singapore in 1996 and I've yet to hear a dissenting voice at a family dinner table when it comes to that everyday issue of raising a penguin chick in Manhattan.

The backlash was unprecedented, if not entirely unexpected. Books and pulping are always uneasy bedfellows. The unfortunate use of the highly emotive "pulp" evokes horrific, grainy images of book-burning rallies in Nazi Germany and other, less salubrious hotspots. The comparison is grossly unfair and illogical, but kneejerk reactions are mostly triggered by emotion, not reason. That's why they instinctively feel right. Rubbish is burned. Art isn't. Thousands of signatures were collected for online petitions and open letters called for the book to be spared. Fellow authors boycotted the Singapore Writers Festival, of which I am a regular participant. Some Singaporeans called for a boycott of the country's public libraries, of which I am a proud ambassador. I was also an author of illustrated children's books. I was also asked privately by a couple of prominent gay activists to take a stand. I was also a staunch supporter of Singapore's public library system. I was also in Brazil. It was awkward.

And then, inevitably, sales spiked. *And Tango Makes Three* was in every newspaper. Its cover graced TV screens and prominent shelves at major bookstores. International journalists fell over themselves to dropkick the latest open goal to make Singapore look ridiculous on the global stage (and, my god, do we give them plenty of goal-scoring opportunities). Without doing a thing, *And Tango Makes Three* could not shift copies fast enough, leaving me with no alternative.

I needed a penguin book ban.

I returned to my lonely, forgotten book and searched for any ambiguous illustrations – a penguin facing another penguin's back, a male penguin smiling lovingly towards another male penguin, a penguin waddling past a rainbow, a couple of penguins organising a Mardi Gras on an ice floe. I'd take anything. I was desperate. But I found nothing. My book was lumbered with the straightest, most heterosexual penguins in history. My work could not be shoehorned into that popular canon of great gay penguin literature.

But the debate raged on. The nuanced attitudes and subtle differences between old and new Singapore had crossed swords once again, only this time the battleground was the most benign of settings – the local library. I felt so sorry for the wonderfully dedicated staff who work tirelessly for the NLB. I know many of them personally and they bore the brunt of a vicious, unrelenting critical response that resulted from a single, misguided decision to try and reflect social norms that can no longer be easily defined or categorised. A reductionist, one-size-fits-all approach is just not applicable in an incredibly complex and rapidly evolving society. Attempts to measure and quantify social norms are understandable, but extremely difficult and perhaps even futile, as Penguin-gate demonstrated. But tarring NLB staff with the same brush, dismissing the fine organisation as a hive of conservative crackpots, was no different to banning a children's book on the grounds that most Singaporeans are conservative crackpots. In this instance, only the penguins were black and white.

Penguin-gate aside, my unstinting admiration for NLB is borne not out of self-interest, but bitter personal experience. If the public library of my childhood downsizes any further, it will be reduced to a torn shoebox filled with muscular, waxed men showing off puffed-out pecs on romance novel covers. Incidentally, where do publishers find those bare-chested men for their romance covers? Those guys are one push-up away from lactating.

When I was a child in Dagenham, the general attitude towards reading was ambivalent at best. But today's working-class children are running out of places to read in England (as I write this, Russell Brand has revealed his intention to donate money to set up a library in his former school in Grays – an Essex neighbour of Dagenham – after learning that the local public library was being relocated). But in Singapore, public reading outlets would simply not be allowed to close. All those on this island are still relevant and innovative, expanding their e-book collections and organising more community events, storytelling sessions and exhibitions than ever before. If you can be proud of nothing else in Singapore, be proud of your public library system.

The civic-minded residents of Queenstown certainly are. They earned their library a late reprieve. Their concerns extended beyond the educational and leisure needs of their children. They fought to preserve their town's heritage. The Queenstown Public Library was the first full-time branch library in the country. Lee Kuan Yew opened the building in April 1970. Queenstown also became the first fully air-conditioned library in 1978. Overseas readers might struggle with the relevance, but at a recent literary festival a reader handed me a book to sign with pages yellower than rotten teeth. The book was less than a decade old and falling to bits. Singapore's merciless humidity has no respect for literature. And its town planners are not always respectful of their heritage.

But in the case of the Queenstown Library, common sense prevailed, thanks to the redoubtable efforts of civic group My Community. Its members lobbied for the conservation of the library, Alexandra Hospital and the famous wet market in Commonwealth Avenue. All were gazetted for conservation in June 2014. Not for the first time, the people pushed back against the number crunchers. And, keep this to yourselves, the people won.

Of course the war rages on. When I stepped out of Queenstown MRT station and onto Commonwealth Avenue, Old Singapore had been pummelled into submission. The cinema, the hawker centre, the supermarket and the other red brick buildings I recall frequenting after Tanjong Pagar games had been replaced with a construction site for a condo project promising integrated convenience just a short MRT ride away from the CBD. There were artists' impressions of the future buildings along the corrugated fencing. What do you make of these artists' impressions? I find them less accurate than my impressions of Donald Duck. The futuristic buildings are invariably surrounded by a pre-Raffles forest canopy and captured at the very moment a flock of geese chose to ignore the migratory route of their ancestors to float past the cloudless sky. Reservoirs and rivers are pulled from nearby communities to flow past the project and the eerily empty footpaths are filled only with smiley, sweat-free, pan-Asian families all carrying balloons. And they're always wearing white, billowing clothes. Do developers pull the best-looking families from PAP conferences?

As I made my way across the boggy turf sandwiched between a couple of construction sites, I saw that the library really was the last memory standing. Tucked away on Margaret Drive, its grey curvy roof and retro bow-tie motif shouted its '70s heritage loudly and proudly. Despite its inaccessible location – hidden behind the condo projects – Queenstown Library was doing brisk business. The café, the study tables and a children's arts and craft workshop were all humming with children and parents. It was a Saturday afternoon. The visitors were not short of entertainment options, but were doing what thousands of Singaporeans do seven days of the week – making use of their local library. I never take such a fine view for granted (some of the grimmest places I've ever visited are musty, sepia-tinted, sparsely-populated local libraries in England and Australia). Queenstown Library even had what every Singaporean library must have by law – an uncle sleeping in the quiet reading room.

If Singapore's first library got a happy ending, then Singapore's biggest library scandal at least got a different ending. The public outcry led to a late reprieve for the penguin book. *And Tango Makes Three* was not pulped in the end. Nor was *The White Swan Express,* which focused on children adopted by straight, gay, mixed-race and single parents. That book was also caught up in the public row. (I'm now considering writing a book about gay black penguins meeting white lesbian swans at the Chingay Parade. It will blow the censors' minds.) The books were moved to the adult section of public libraries, in the best interests of our family values. For heaven's sake, don't tell anyone about Snow White. She's unmarried and lives with seven dwarves. The woman's depraved.

Queenstown was home to Singapore's first community sports complex with stadium on the left and swimming pool on the right. Queenstown Stadium, once hosted Tanjong Pagar United and me on a megaphone. Hopefully, Tanjong Pagar will return.

Queenstown Library is Singapore's first library and it also stocks my children's book on penguins. It isn't banned. Sadly.

At least someone has taken care with the vibrant murals at Singapore's first HDB flats.

Eleven

FOR A LONG TIME, Pulau Hantu piqued my interest. The island is remote, uninhabited and, in the context of Singapore's Southern Islands, distant. Look at a map. It's tucked away behind Pulau Bukom's cluster of islands, out of sight and almost entirely out of mind. Unlike the more popular islands off Sentosa, Pulau Hantu doesn't really register. It could be the name. That was the other reason for my interest. Ghost Island. Pulau Hantu means ghost island in Malay. It's hardly welcoming. But the isolation appealed to me. Here was an island with an obvious connection to Old Singapore, a rare example of an undisturbed location little different to how it might have presented itself to Raffles. (I soon discovered I was entirely wrong about that.) In other words, there was the alluring idea of going where so few Singaporeans had gone before. That was incentive enough. And again, the place was called Ghost Island. We live in a country where our literal sensibilities extend to naming open spaces... open spaces. (Hang your head in shame, the Penang Road Open Space.) So Ghost Island suggested a genuine walk on the wild side.

First I had to get there. Bumboats and sampans do not provide scheduled services from the mainland. And so it came to pass that I found myself bouncing along the waves of East Jurong Channel with an affable Italian called Alessandro who kept handing me laxatives disguised as underwater photos of angry sharks nose-butting scuba divers.

Whilst researching Pulau Hantu, I came across the inestimable Debby Ng and her band of Hantu Bloggers. Back in 2004, Debby organised her first group diving trip off the island to explore its reefs and the response was so overwhelming that she formed The Hantu Bloggers. Today, the non-profit dive organisation, run by volunteers, conducts regular dives to raise awareness of the biologically diverse reefs and monitor their health. They represent an expanding group of younger Singaporeans with a growing interest in their environment beyond the rice bowl. So I signed up for a dive, despite the nagging drawback that I cannot dive for health reasons.

Early in 2014, I punctured a lung. It wasn't a road accident or a dramatic act of heroism. I had laughed too much. I didn't believe the specialist either. According to the doctor, tall people with elongated organs are more susceptible to tiny tears and perforations in their lungs through sudden movements. During an appearance on a TV show, I had laughed and felt a constricting, tightening pain inside my chest. An X-ray later revealed the tear. I punctured my lung by laughing.

I'm not entirely sure Debby believed me either. As the sturdy vessel *Dolphin Explorer* powered away from West Coast Pier, she nodded as I explained the laughing punctured lung thing. She comforted me by suggesting that I might see some marine life in the lagoon, like a parent reassuring a cowardly kid there is just as much fun on the choo-choo train as there is on the roller-coaster.

She produced a photo album and gave a brief lecture on the marine life found around Pulau Hantu.

"This is coral," she said. "This is actually a living animal that lives at the bottom of the sea."

I peered up from my notepad.

"Hey, I know I said I've never dived before, but I know what coral is," I insisted, nursing my bruised pride. "I'm not that bad."

"Oh, I'm really sorry," she interjected. "It's just that we get a lot of real beginners on these diving trips and I never know what the knowledge level is going to be."

"Well, you don't have to worry about me on that score. I'm really not that bad."

"That's great. OK, this is a giant carpet anemone."

I stared at her.

"OK, I am that bad."

As we sped towards Pulau Hantu, the rest of the group rigged up quickly, like a montage of quick cuts from a Batman movie. Suits were pulled on, weight belts tightened, tubes and taps adjusted, oxygen tanks rolled into place and pressure gauges checked.

I blew down my snorkel tube to make sure there was no sand in it.

I gestured towards the oxygen tanks securely packed in a metal case and commented that if we encountered a great white shark we had the means to blow it up. A couple of the divers wondered if I was out my depth with a snorkel.

But the shark talk drew in Alessandro. An experienced, international diver, the kind Italian empathised with my diving virginity and sought to reassure me by highlighting his near misses with sea creatures who eat people.

"Ah, you see that photo there, that's a blue shark, look at its teeth," he said, grinning with the paternal pride of a new dad handing out baby snaps. "That was a clear day in South Africa. But going in with sharks when the water's murky is no good. It can be irritating to bump into a shark. It can spoil the dive, you know."

My wariness wasn't helped by the skipper's peerless efforts to make the crossing in a vertical position. The boat's nose had an aversion to water. And yet, as the mainland slipped away, I could not stop smiling.

"It's fun, right?" Debby said, appearing at my side.

"It's 8am on a Sunday morning. I wouldn't want to be anywhere else," I replied truthfully.

As we zipped past the container ships, she detailed the etymology of the island. The Hantu Bloggers had interviewed former inhabitants of Pulau Hantu who offered a rather anti-climactic explanation. In the 1950s, owls populated the island and their distinct ghostly hooting led to locals coming up with the name. In the 1970s, the island was a popular stopping-off point to exchange contraband, so authorities were keen to play up the Ghost Island element to potentially scare away the illegal trade.

"Those are the theories we have for Ghost Island," Debby said. "Oh and we'll have to drop you off at the jetty and leave you there. So you might have the island to yourself."

Alas, I didn't. As *Dolphin Explorer* zoomed off towards the nearby reefs, I passed a couple of fishermen on the jetty and discovered a near-naked uncle washing some camping pots and pans in a toilet sink. His skimpy shorts left little to the imagination – or wiggle room. At times, I thought I was being winked at.

"Can I ask why you are here?" I said, washing my hands beside him.

"Washing pots lah," he replied.

He was an affable, pot-bellied Chinese chap with a sun-crisp skin tone.

"No, I meant here at Pulau Hantu."

"Oh, camping. We go camping to different islands, friends, family, show them my Singapore from last time."

I wanted to hug him, but I refrained. Hugging a near-naked man on a near-deserted island can give the wrong impression.

"So I won't have the island to myself. I liked the idea of having my own island."

"It's OK, what," he said, scrubbing a saucepan with wire wool. "Can swim to the smaller island. That one definitely got no people."

Feeling all Robinson Crusoe, I took his advice. I passed his camping group near the tiny beach. There were about 20 of them, spread across half a dozen tents, with coffee and instant noodles boiling on portable stoves and damp washing strung out on lines tied between two palm trees. Pulau Hantu made Pulau Ubin look like Orchard Road the night before Christmas. For that reason, everyone greets each other. With the regal air of a visiting dignitary, I waved to every camper. They all reciprocated. Strangers sitting nearby in foldable deck chairs muttered their "hellos" and "good mornings". Consider eyeballing every passer-by at Raffles Place and delivering a hearty "good morning". Someone would send for a straitjacket.

I dumped my bag, socks and trainers in a shady spot beneath a coconut tree and covered them with dry leaves. I stood at the edge of big Pulau Hantu and peered across at little Pulau Hantu. In the mid-70s, land reclamation had increased the size of both Pulau Hantu Besar (Big Ghost Island) and Pulau Hantu Kecil (Little Ghost Island), pulling them closer together. The expansions left a narrower strip between them, a shallow lagoon to wade across at low tide.

It was not low tide.

But the distance was swimmable, somewhere between 50m to 100m from sandbank to sandbank. I plunged into the calm, reasonably clear waters and figured three to four lengths of an average swimming pool could be successfully navigated. But

Singapore's currents are deceptively strong. They had offered a very public display of their mightiness when the *Dolphin Explorer* had struggled to dock at the jetty, the currents continually pushing the vessel away from the island. The halfway point presented a fascinating optical illusion. My arms and legs were stroking and kicking in a reasonably coordinated fashion, but the shoreline was stubbornly refusing to move. It wasn't retreating, but it wasn't getting any closer either. I felt anchored in the middle of the lagoon, which was adequately protected by a rock bund, but still reasonably close to the open sea. I tried to touch the bottom, which was an ill-advised move. The toes at the end of my frame failed to find any sand and, as I slipped beneath the water, I saw Alessandro's blue shark and heard John Williams' *Jaws* theme. Not literally. That would've been weird. But I was very much aware of my solitude. Snorkelling was out. I needed a sense of direction. I had this daft idea of ducking my head to admire some coral through the sediment-stained lagoon and then looking up to see the coast of Batam. Powered by images of Alessandro's blue shark, which strangely helped, I opted for a finishing kick and eventually flopped onto the beach of Pulau Hantu Kecil.

And this time, I really was alone. I had the little ghost island to myself. Pulau Hantu Kecil lived up to its name. The island was tiny, little more than a green speck beneath Pulau Bukom, but to be the only inhabitant was a liberating experience. A Singaporean island belonged entirely to me, which was handy as I was bare-footed and stumbling through the thorny, prickly undergrowth like a squealing idiot. But a soothing chorus of cicadas accompanied my pitiful squeals. Kingfishers floated from tree to tree and a pair of kites kept me company overhead, perusing the lagoon menu. Being the only person was exhilarating. I started shouting and singing, loudly, for no other reason than I could. Then I took to bellowing "Wilson" repeatedly. Climbing over branches, stepping around near-horizontal trees stretching towards the sea, wading waist deep in the lagoon to avoid jagged rocks and the unavoidable washed-up trash was topped only by me reaching a clearing and shouting: "Wilson!... Wilson!" For an hour, I was a genuine castaway, Tom Hanks without the straggly hair. Or at least, I thought I was until I glanced over my shoulder and noticed that my demented cries had attracted the attention of a fellow foreign worker hanging out his washing on Pulau Bukom.

The illusion of island solitude could only be maintained if I turned my back on Pulau Bukom's bustling, grinding and spectacularly ugly petrochemical installations. Some call the place Shell Island as it houses the company's oil refinery and plays a pivotal role in Singapore (and the region's) economy. But that also makes it a clunking, silence-shattering blot on a pristine landscape. The refinery's endless drone of trundling lorries, industrious factories and reclamation works was a tiresome distraction. Pulau Hantu Kecil was a picturesque little spot for quiet contemplation. Just don't turn around.

WITH THE TIDE RECEDING, the return swim was more agreeable. I shook the red ant fortress from my bag, shoes and socks and had a gander around Pulau Hantu Besar. The campers had gone home. The bigger island now belonged to me. I was annexing my way towards the mainland. On closer inspection, Pulau Hantu was more artificial than I had hoped. The hand of the urban planner was always visible. The coconut and the casuarina trees were lined up neatly. Mother Nature is far more erratic and anarchic. The last of her work was found in a small patch of mangrove at the island's summit. There were around 10 wooden shelters, some barbecue pits, a toilet and a couple of lagoons carved into the reclaimed land. Clearly, Pulau Hantu was earmarked for a purpose beyond providing an attractive spot for fishermen and overnight campers.

And then I found it. Or, at least, I heard it. There was an incessant thwacking. I looked up from my notepad and noticed, some 30m away, a Caucasian chap helping himself to wooden logs that had been carefully placed around the island's last remaining mangrove to act as a protective border. He was hacking away at a log with an axe. Well, I say axe, but it was more of a toothpick. After dozens of blunt axe chops, the small log eventually took pity and split its sides to end the poor man's torment. Delighted with his Tarzan-like taming of the jungle, the Axe Man of Ghost Island then dropped his splintered pieces into a wheelbarrow. Questions flooded the brain. Where did he come from? Why was he vandalising a perfectly adequate log border around the mangrove? Why was he using an axe less threatening than a nail file? And where did the wheelbarrow come from? Did he bring it with him or was it left on the island for passing axe nutters?

I had no choice but to follow him. And the answers arrived in the anti-climactic shape of a pleasure craft anchored in the lagoon. They had even found their way to Pulau Hantu. I watched Axe Man attempt to make fire, standing over a barbeque, fanning the non-existent flames from his wooden splinters with one hand and holding a Tiger beer in the other. A couple of women stood at his side, sipping wine and nodding appreciatively as Man made fire. My fantasy island now had all the exotic mystique of a condo barbecue.

So I went snorkelling.

Expecting to see nothing but rusty beer cans and Pringles tubes, I stripped off, shoved the snorkel on and slipped into the warm waters of Pulau Hantu Besar. Well, every expectation was exceeded. The sediment was everywhere, suspended in the water like sandy string, but the visibility was still around 1.5m. And there were fish, so many fish of all shapes, colours and stripes. Following the rock bund, I paddled over schools of blue fish and what I think were anemone fish (like the stripy clown fish in *Finding Nemo*). I am not going to pretend the lagoon was pellucid and a mirror image of the tropical paradise found off the coast of Tioman Island. My snorkelling was often interrupted as a passing piece of driftwood whacked me in the ear. Litter was an issue and the water was murky, but I could mostly see the sandy bottom as the fish darted around, playing peekaboo along the rock bund.

Even under the water, I kept thinking, "this is Singapore". This is a country where the sea off the East Coast Park is so dark, polluted and uninviting that we won't even get in to pee (I must say I had a stupendous pee in the lagoon – the puffy, yellowy cloud was a glorious sight to behold). Even dogs turn their noses up at our surrounding seas. I've often seen tongue-flapping canines scamper across the East Coast Park beach with unbridled joy etched across their faces, only to stop suddenly at the water's edge. They paw at the foamy sludge with a horrified look that seems to say: "I might lick my own balls, but I'm not going in there."

And yet here I was playing hide and seek with tropical fish, their vibrant yellows and blues glimmering in the sunlight. Finding the tiniest pocket of Old Singapore on dry land is difficult enough, so discovering one on the seabed was a real highlight.

And Old Singaporeans surrounded me. Locals can still afford seafront dwellings at Pulau Hantu. These waters host more than 250 species of native hard corals. I don't think I saw any of them. I spotted lots of bright fish I mostly failed to identify. But I was in no hurry to leave.

I might still be there had I not been disturbed by a faint buzzing. I squinted through my goggles and sighed. The divers had sent a boat to rescue me. A smaller vessel, a glorified dinghy really, puttered past in the lagoon. A young Chinese guy with snake-like hips, a disturbingly deep tan and naked but for an orange sarong that somehow suited him, waved at me from the boat.

"Come, you struggling, I take you back," said my apparent rescuer, young enough to be my son.

"I'm fine," I hissed, quite literally. I was still breathing through my snorkel.

"No lah, you tired already, I take you back to the big boat, in case cannot make it."

"But still got time before they finish their dive," I insisted.

"Never mind, you come back first, rest on the big boat, those ones are good swimmers."

With my nose firmly out of joint, I thrashed and splashed my way back to his floating phallic symbol. I registered my dissatisfaction with melodramatic eye rolls, which Popeye the Sarong Man missed entirely because I was still wearing my steamed-up goggles.

To compound my humiliation, he leaned over the boat, smiled, and offered a hand. The vessel was small and low and anchored in shin-deep water.

"Come I lift you," he said.

"No, no, it's quite all right, thank you," I insisted, turning all polite PG Wodehouse in my offended sensibilities. "I'm quite capable of climbing into your boat, thank you very much."

I splashed a long right leg through the air and landed with a thud on top of the narrow, wooden bow – at the very moment a mischievous wave lapped against the side of the boat, causing it to lurch to its right side. My side. My soaked shorts and rash vest suddenly turned into a lubricant. The bow turned into a slide.

I slipped off the boat like a chicken sausage.

Coughing and sputtering in the shallow water, I laughed off any remaining dignity and said: "Yeah, all right, give us a hand into your bloody boat."

We were firm friends after that.

Back on the boat, the divers returned, unloaded and then settled down to share big fish stories. Less than 100m from where I was edging along the rock bund, they had photographed sea slugs, a turtle, cuttlefish, a bamboo shark and a pair of shark's eggs. And then Debby turned towards me.

"And did you see anything, Neil?"

I fiddled with my goggles strap and muttered: "I saw some yellow fish and some blue fish and some stripy black and white fish."

I sounded like a playgroup kid describing his painting.

With commendable patience, Debby smiled at my scribbled drawings and suggested I had encountered a yellow soap fish among others. I felt a real sense of accomplishment. She had validated me. I had swum with the fishes. I had even swum reasonably close to the sharks (and their eggs). The Hantu Bloggers had rubberstamped my credentials as an intrepid explorer.

As the West Coast Pier crept closer on the horizon, I listened intently to their latest coral reef discoveries and their plans to upload photo galleries and blog posts to spread awareness. They spoke of upcoming conservation projects, meetings and strategic goals. Their can-do optimism was infectious and invigorating. They exuded positivity. Mostly in their 20s and early 30s, their respect for Old Singapore gives New Singapore a fighting chance.

They had been more than accommodating, understanding hosts. They had organised one of the best days I had ever spent in Singapore.

For an hour, I had Pulau Hantu Kecil, an entire Singaporean island, to myself. I didn't have a volleyball, but I did shout "Wilson" quite a lot.

At Pulau Hantu Besar, I went snorkelling for the first time in Singaporean waters. I saw lots of fish. I also fell off the boat.

Twelve

I ONCE CONSIDERED buying the worst tourist attraction in Britain. In 2012, the Louis Tussauds House of Wax closed down due to the failing health of its elderly owners and, more pertinently perhaps, for having the world's worst waxwork collection, as determined by just about anyone foolish enough to pay a fiver to visit the museum. I loved the place so much I went twice. Louis Tussauds House of Wax was in the Suffolk seaside town of Great Yarmouth. On a map of the United Kingdom, Great Yarmouth is the bit that sticks out, the buttocks, and the windiest area, too. Family photos on a Great Yarmouth beach depict families looking like war refugees. We have photos of my teary-eyed, blue-faced daughter holding a candy floss stick with her blurred father chasing a disappearing pink cloud in the background.

That's how Louis Tussauds House of Wax presumably got unsuspecting fools through the door, to escape the howling winds. With a degree of pride, I can say with some authority that no other country in the world would tolerate a tourist attraction so spectacularly crap as Great Yarmouth's waxwork museum. For 57 years, visitors paid to admire a sun-tanned Adolf Hitler, an orange Sean Connery, a middle-aged Michael Owen, a Borat-influenced Daley Thompson and, most offensively of all, a youthful Prince

Charles standing with Princess Diana. When I last visited, the royals were still placed together despite the fact that they bore no resemblance to the real people, Charles had remarried and poor Diana had died. Naturally, Louis Tussauds became a cult attraction, a waxwork museum where not one model bore so much as a passing resemblance to the person it allegedly represented. I had a soft spot for the faded, musty attraction because of its sheer British eccentricity and its spectacular defiance of modern tastes.

And in 2012, the owners couldn't find a buyer for the museum. I read the story online (the House of Wax had developed a cult following across the world, such was its crapness) and ran to my wife in the living room.

"You remember that waxwork museum in Great Yarmouth, the really terrible one?" I shouted. "I'm gonna buy it."

"Of course you are," she replied, not looking up from her phone.

"I'm serious. They've got 150 waxwork figures, they're worth £100 each, plus there's the value of the business. It might only be £50,000 to £100, 000."

"But you haven't got that kind of money."

"What if I got a loan? Singapore is supposed to be encouraging entrepreneurialism and new business start-ups."

She put down her Candy Crush game. This was serious.

"Neil, a Singapore bank is not going to lend you the money to buy the world's worst waxwork museum in another country."

She had a point. But I seriously considered my financial options for a couple of hours before concluding that buying a genuinely unsettling waxwork figure of Mr Bean was not a sound investment. Sadly, the entire waxwork collection was eventually sold for an undisclosed sum to a fellow lunatic in the Czech Republic (where I bet he's making a killing) and the Great Yarmouth property was put up for sale.

Louis Tussauds House of Wax was special because it was an oddball and we need more oddballs in an increasingly drab world of corporate control. With Sentosa on a mission to maximise its revenue from every square inch of an already saturated island, it's hard not to conclude that Singapore takes itself – and its finances – far too seriously to entertain such a cultural oddity.

Thankfully, Haw Par Villa is the nutty exception. It's mad, slightly unhinged and overwhelmingly rubbish. Without a doubt, Haw Par Villa is the Louis Tussauds House of Wax of Singapore. There is no higher compliment. The Tiger Balm Gardens are not only Old Singapore. They are oddball Singapore. In 2013, *The Guardian* called Haw Par Villa "the theme park made in hell". Like the sorely missed House of Wax, the Pasir Panjang freakshow also made global headlines for the silliest reasons. I hadn't visited in 10 years and wondered if Haw Par Villa was destined to share the same fate as my favourite waxwork museum. Certainly, the setting had already changed. I arrived at an MRT station, via an MRT line, that didn't exist a decade ago. As I marched purposefully up the villa's slope at its entrance, I sincerely hoped that nothing else had changed beyond a neighbouring MRT station. For its own sake, Haw Par Villa still had to be terrible, macabre, distasteful and offensive.

Luckily, it was. It really was. To summarise very briefly – as there is still a handful of Singaporeans, expats and tourists who haven't yet visited, an inexcusable crime in itself – Haw Par Villa is a theme park filled with more than 1,000 statues and dioramas devoted to Chinese mythology. The greatest Buddhist, Confucian and Taoist tales are displayed in all their disembowelled gory. Basking in their Tiger Balm ointment wealth, the brothers Aw Boon Haw and Aw Boon Par built the most ostentatious seafront property with gardens devoted to the ghastly, blood-dripping exhibition on morality and crime and punishment. In 1937, Haw

Par Villa cost around $1 million. Today, $1 million will cover a sea-facing HDB flat at Marine Terrace.

Strolling around the decaying theme park, which was near deserted despite the free admission, the old favourites remained. In the broad thriftiness and virtues tableau, children were encouraged to respect the value of hard work and law and order by admiring a thief getting his teeth pulled out, a policeman punching a gangster repeatedly in his bloodied, pulpy forehead and a loan shark settling an unpaid debt in an unorthodox fashion. First he took the debtor's pig. Then he took the debtor's wife. That's just too much. Take a man's wife, by all means, but never take another man's pig.

Wandering around, the obvious neglect was depressing. Haw Par Villa was in serious disrepair. Cracked tiles and pathways allowed the weeds to poke through, mould-stained stone benches with peeling Fujifilm signs hardly encouraged anyone to use them and many of the statues and displays needed at the very least a fresh coat of paint. The gift shop was closed, as was the food court and parts of the park. Its heritage Hua Song Museum was shut down in 2012. Whether anyone actually cares is another matter. I counted less than a dozen other visitors while I was there, a Singaporean family, a lone Caucasian and some curious tourists from China. The only noise came from a gardener, who had armed himself with a leaf blower and was pushing piles of leaves in circles around the Aw memorials. His work appeared pointless, but he seemed to be enjoying himself.

Thankfully, the iconic Ten Courts of Hell remained open. There cannot be many Singaporeans over the age of say, 30, who do not have a vivid memory of visiting the Ten Courts of Hell. The tableau of hellish retribution isn't easily forgotten. It's the most terrifying tourist attraction since Louis Tussauds' waxwork figure of Cliff Richard. At the entrance, a sign recommended "prarental guidance". Even the spelling was scary at Haw Par Villa.

Inside the darkened, ghoulish exhibition of eternal punishment in the afterlife, the images of burning bodies and decapitated heads were only marginally less affecting than watching a Chinese mother provide commentary for her two wide-eyed young children. At the Seventh Court of Hell, she pointed at the hideous sculpture and said: "Ah, read that one ah... Rumour mongers... People who make up stories get their tongues pulled out. You see? Mustn't make up stories one." At the Sixth Court of Hell, however, guilty folks were being sawn into two for the heinous crime of misusing books. I'm all for that.

And I'm all for Haw Par Villa. Universal Studios and the gardens at Marina Bay have their place, but they're distinctly un-Singaporean in their appeal. I had a great time at Universal Studios in both Singapore and Florida, but there is little to choose between them beyond the harsh reality that Florida offered more attractions (but was more expensive). Likewise, Gardens by the Bay is a welcome, artificial antidote to the ceaseless construction around Keppel Harbour, but it's little different to the green spaces offered in other sprawling cities.

But Haw Par Villa is as Singaporean as Singlish. Incomprehensible to some and just plain daft to others, Haw Par Villa is viewed with a degree of confusion and bemusement by outsiders but instantly recognised and understood by almost every Singaporean. Every country has a theme park of some description. Only Singapore has Haw Par Villa. It's silly, inefficient, old-fashioned, weird and makes no money. It's the anti-tourist attraction in a modern economy, entirely anathema to New Singapore. The macabre oddity practically raises a middle finger to town planners and number crunchers. And it will always have more of a Singaporean soul than an American theme park designed in the United States and financed by a Malaysian casino operator.

So I'll leave you where I left my Chinese family, in front of Haw Par Villa's most infamous sculpture – the one of a lactating woman breastfeeding a wrinkled grandmother. The truly terrifying image may be championing traditional Asian values and the need to care for our elderly, but it still came across as a perverted endorsement of necrophilia. Still, that didn't stop the Chinese family. The guy gathered his wife and children and herded them together in front of the sculpture. And they all smiled for his camera. That's the family Christmas card taken care of.

WITH THE MEMORY of giggling kids posing in front of a suckling grandmother seared into my soul forever, I took the MRT to One-North and then the No. 191 feeder bus along Portsdown Road in search of a literal taste of my East London childhood.

Before my late grandfather chained me to the kitchen sideboard of his café and ordered me to butter sliced loaves for the best part of a decade, he ran an industrial canteen in the bowels of a London factory. Like Singapore's indefatigable hawkers, he served hundreds of people every day without seeing sunlight. On one terrible occasion, his thriving business came to a standstill, thanks to a wanton act of vandalism.

Now he's gone, it's probably safe to admit that I was the vandal.

During the school holidays, my mother took me to another world beyond the red-brick housing estate of Dagenham. We travelled less than 10 miles on the Tube to the City of London, where the dizzying streets were filled with men in suits. Where I grew up, men only wore suits for weddings and funerals. As we passed along the city's historic cobbled footpaths, my mother stopped and invited me to peer through a rusted, iron grille door built into the side of brick wall. On the other side was a darkened staircase leading into a subterranean jungle of blue-collar workers, production lines, deep-fat fryers and the permanent aroma of sizzling bacon.

"That's your granddad's canteen," she said.

"Wow," I said, leaning against the iron door.

"Fuck," my mother said as I accidentally pushed the iron door through its frame.

"What did you lean on it for?" she shouted, as the world's oldest, rustiest, heaviest door clattered and clunked its way down the staircase before smashing into a pinball machine. "It's not a door. It's a fire escape."

"But you told me to have a look at my granddad's canteen," I whimpered.

"Yes, but I didn't tell you to smash the place up, did I? Come on," she ordered, dragging me along the cobbles and past the appalled faces of liberal office workers from the leafier environs of London, where it was less common to see indomitable working-class women dragging their wailing offspring along by the ear.

"Leave all the lying to me."

Of course, when we arrived at the canteen, my granddad and his staff were still sweeping up the broken mess. Everyone was in shock. Someone had just shoved a cast iron door down the stairs. Granddad shook his head wearily, unable to grasp the nihilistic tendencies of modern youth and its thirst for random destruction.

"In 20 years, this has never happened," he muttered in disbelief, before turning to me. "Did you see anyone near the fire escape, Neil?"

"Nah, we didn't see anyone, did we, Neil?" my mother interjected.

"Er, no," I lied, staring down at my upturned palms, covered in incriminating grease from the fire escape grille.

"Hooligans," Granddad mumbled breathlessly, heaving the cast iron door back up the staircase.

"Hooligans," my mother concurred.

"Hooligans," I added for grown-up gravitas, whilst dragging my stained hands down the back of my trousers.

The factory was closed down shortly after and my granddad used the redundancy payout to set up the café where I spent all of my formative years washing dishes and being abused by Cockney labourers. But the canteen left me with powerful memories of a family-run workplace. Husbands, wives, sisters, sons, daughters and in-laws all worked together, argued together and lied together when an idiot grandson pushed an iron door down a staircase. I never expected to see anything quite like my family's long-since-demolished blue-collar canteen again. I certainly didn't anticipate finding one in a Singaporean forest.

But as I entered the isolated, exclusive black and white bungalow community of the Wessex Estate and ducked down Whitchurch Road, I rediscovered my childhood. I found my family-run East London canteen. It was called Colbar, one of Old Singapore's finest feel-good stories.

In 1953, a simple two-unit eating house was opened in Jalan Hang Jebat to cater to both Singaporeans and British military personnel, serving the most eclectic menu long before fusion food became fashionable. Singaporeans came for the *hor fun*. The Brits came from all over the island for what was considered to be the best liver and onions in Singapore. Everyone came to Colbar. Then like so many successful Singaporean heritage stories, the bulldozers intervened. With impeccable timing, the old Colbar was torn down in 2003 – the year of its 50th birthday – to make way for a wider road to link the Ayer Rajah Expressway (AYE) to Portsdown Road. But this heritage tale had a happy ending of sorts. The local community rallied and received sufficient backing from all the relevant authorities to rebuild Colbar – using some of the original, salvaged materials – at a nearby site in Whitchurch Road. Colbar's resurrection was an early success for civic engagement.

Accompanied only by cicadas, I followed the rickety path to 9A Whitchurch Road and found the 1950s. The nondescript single-storey building stood out like the wonderful relic it was among the swankier (I might have accidentally added an 's' there) eateries of the Wessex Estate. The blue and white painted wooden panels were covered in kitsch, as were all canteens of that time, including my grandfather's. Old photographs of customers and their local football teams across the decades filled the turquoise-coloured walls, a retro set of weighing scales greeted visitors at the entrance, dusty cupboards were cluttered with old trophies and knickknacks and an old, analog TV sat at the end of the longish wooden counter. And it was a Singaporean family-run business serving no-frills breakfasts and lunches to diners from all walks of life. All that was missing was my grandmother screaming at my granddad in the kitchen.

As I was essentially at an East London café hidden in a Singaporean forest not far from the Southern Ridges, I ordered egg, chips and beans. I noted that the guy dumped HP sauce and salt and vinegar on my table without being asked, then handed Maggi chilli sauce to a couple of Singaporeans at the next table, again without being asked. Mild stereotypes aside, I savoured the experience of dining at the most picturesque coffee shop in Singapore. Sitting on the terrace and surrounded by lush, breezy greenery, I noticed the lack of air-conditioning. It wasn't needed. White-collared Singaporeans and expats from the nearby media industries sat shoulder to shoulder on plastic chairs and no one really perspired. They talked shop while *hor fun* gravy and egg yolk dribbled down their chins. It was quite a sight.

Of course, Colbar was an old gem in every sense. Its reasonable prices still appealed to Singaporeans. With crushing inevitability, the rest of the Wessex Estate had succumbed to the highest bidder, a depressingly dull home to Ferraris and tai tais. Across the road from Colbar, a European restaurant was doing a roaring trade among the well-heeled (with scarcely a Singaporean among them). While I waited for the No. 191 feeder bus (a tokenistic nod towards the commoner; the Wessex Estate is really only accessible by car) after my lunch, a couple of plump guys roared past me in a black BMW with the roof down, presumably to make room for their heads. They parked on double yellow lines, being proper hard men and all, squeezed their frames out of the sports car and waddled towards the restaurant. They left the BMW's red leather seats to melt in the midday sunshine, which confirmed the old adage that money can buy a parking space on double yellow lines but it cannot spare a scorched arse.

The scene was entirely at odds with the simple charms of the historic Colbar Café and its good grub catering to all, just across the road. The guys swaggered past me, pleased with themselves and their broiling BMW front and centre of the restaurant. In such instances, first impressions are everything. Snap judgments are unavoidable. Some will see sophisticated guys, successful, aspirational, a fast car for fast lives. But I will always see two tubby guys with exceedingly small willies.

According to this Haw Par Villa exhibit, those who misuse books should be sawn in two as punishment. I'm all for it.

Colbar Café is an East London café set in a Singaporean forest. It's weird, wonderful and does a damn good fry-up.

Thirteen

I WILL NOT allow the suburban shopping malls of Old Singapore to die. If they go, they will take their priceless health clinics with them and that cannot happen. Their old-school marketing campaigns are uniquely Singaporean. More importantly, they are insane. Nothing says traditional shopping centre quite like a blown-up, graphic poster of a weeping sphincter.

For many years now, I have trawled the neglected, decaying malls of heartland Singapore, making my way past the "mom and pop" family-run businesses to find the clinic promising to cure the most dreadful ailments in glorious technicolour. I was reminded of their surreal uniqueness when I visited Rochor Centre, where a traditional Chinese medicine centre promised to cure everything from diarrhoea to memory loss (are these people forgetting where the toilet is?). With each fresh discovery, I hope to learn of a new disease, preferably one that comes with an explanatory poster displaying the symptoms. At Rochor Centre, the clinic promised to cure Herpes Zoster, which sounds like the name of a West Ham United striker but, alas, is merely a less common term for shingles.

Happily, the Herbal Beauty Skin Care clinic at Beauty World Centre ticked my box. I was delighted to stand before a poster of a misguided girl having a worm surgically removed from her face.

I had found a new ailment. The clinic vowed to "remove worms in the skin" and had the gory poster to prove it. I wondered where the invisible line of bad taste was drawn at such clinics. What ailments are considered suitable for a graphic display? I've seen posters of the most dreadful symptoms for eczema, acne, chicken pox, weeping sphincters and now facial worms in shop windows. Presumably, penis extensions would be considered beyond the pale. And yet, my daughter can pass a poster of herpes zoster.

Certainly, the marketing logic cannot be faulted. Travel agents put up posters of Disneyland. Suburban beauty clinics stick up pictures of sore arses. It's a transparent, familiar business practice in Singapore. What you see is most definitely what you get. There's no sugarcoating in an old-school clinic. Pick out an ailment in the shop window. Step inside. Bend over. Clench.

To the outsider, the attitude towards embarrassing medical complaints can appear abrasive and tactless, but I've always found the no-nonsense approach strangely endearing and certainly entertaining.

A couple of years ago, my infrequent running along East Coast Park caused some unfortunate chafing between the upper thigh and the undercarriage, so I popped along to the nearest pharmacy, whispered my symptoms and waited for the pharmacist to return. In the meantime, a lovely woman in the queue recognised me and explained that her late mother had enjoyed my early Singapore books, reading them right up until her death. There was a long, uncomfortable pause. I was humbled, obviously, unable to find the appropriate words. Fortunately, the pharmacist found them for me.

"Ah, Mr Humphreys," he bellowed. "Here's the cream for your groin rash."

But our established shopping malls are losing their quirkiness. When I lived in Toa Payoh, my local medical clinic was – and remains – the only clinic I'd ever come across that treated all common ailments, illnesses and sexually transmitted diseases and also offered a very reasonable ear-piercing service. But these places are succumbing to the retail behemoths marching across the island.

A similar fate probably awaits the longstanding tenants of the Beauty World complex. Both Beauty World Centre and its neighbouring Beauty World Plaza in Upper Bukit Timah Road do not fit New Singapore's retail template. Their design is impractical. Beauty World Plaza is too small and Beauty World Centre has escalators jutting out in the middle, so there is not enough atrium space to run endless roadshows hosted by insufferable MCs urging everyone in "da Beauty World house" to "make some noise". And brand franchises are conspicuous by their absence.

The shops are also different. There are interior design showrooms for the landed gentry of Bukit Timah, a fresh flower shop, a roof-top open-air hawker centre (the first I'd come across) and a well-known father-and-son barber shop with the same clientele and retro décor after 30 years.

Outside the sports goods store in Beauty World Plaza, the proprietor was sitting on a leather stool, stringing a racquet.

"I do about four racquets a day," he told me. "Still got good business. Last time I do the parents' racquets. Now I do their children's racquets."

His family-run business set up shop in Beauty World Plaza more than 30 years ago. Now empty glass shells and shop fronts covered in faded newspaper surrounded him. Along with the barber, he was one of the few proprietors left in the ghostly shopping centre. Beauty World was obviously dying, but should anyone care? Why are so many heritage blogs and posts devoted to an antiquated, impractical shopping mall in an overlooked corner of Bukit Timah?

McDonald's, of all places, offered an answer. In early 2014, McDonald's at King Albert Park, not far from Beauty World, was closed down to make way for another high-rise residential project in a prestigious postcode. The public outpouring of emotion on social media took many, including myself, by surprise. So I made a flippant comment about the loss of a fast food outlet hardly equating to the demise of Bukit Brown Cemetery and found myself accused of missing the point. And I had. It wasn't about the burgers. They are still being flipped around Bukit Timah. It was about the building. The building mattered. Thanks to its unusual, almost isolated location, McDonald's Place, with its eateries and supermarket, was a place for students to study, for family breakfasts and dinners, for blind dates and first kisses, for business meetings and job interviews and for nature enthusiasts and dog walkers; it was many things to many people. And now it's gone.

Singaporeans are increasingly realising that you can miss what you once had.

Hopefully, Beauty World will be spared. The roadworks outside are a double-edged sword. They will bring a new MRT line to the shopping centre's doorstep. They will also bring inflated expectations and perhaps a demand for something more than just a retro barber shop. But less really is more when one considers the alternative. Take ION Orchard (please, take it anywhere you like). If there is a more eye-gougingly dull place than this vulgar temple to greed, then for heaven's sake keep it to yourself. Venture inside and you immediately leave Singapore and step into London, Sydney, Shanghai, KL and… you get the boring picture. It's a mall predominantly staffed by poorer Singaporeans and foreigners to serve extraordinarily rich foreigners. I'd rather let the Beauty World barber loose on my neck with a cut-throat razor.

Beauty World is Singaporean. That's all. It's not about old or new Singapore. It's about a country's messy, sprawling, natural, cultural roots. From its family-run flower shops to a surreal beauty clinic promising to remove facial worms, Beauty World is a walk-in memory bank for communities past and present. The shopping complex still connects. ION Orchard, on the other hand, feels less Singaporean than a Prada handbag.

OUT OF BREATH, I threw down my rucksack. The smartly dressed man behind the counter tapped his watch.

"What time you call this," he said.

"Yeah, sorry, I just come from Beauty World. I forgot how long Upper Bukit Timah Road was," I muttered rather sheepishly. "Still got time to look around?"

"Yeah, yeah, yeah," he giggled.

I checked the ticket prices on the counter. My eyes lit up. "Ah, I'm a Singapore resident. So is it free for me?"

"Yeah, yeah, yeah," he said again, still giggling. "You PR, is it?"

"Not quite, in the process."

"Then must pay, $3, yeah, yeah, yeah," he said, swaying gently from side to side and still nodding down at me. "Why you come so late ah, closing in one hour you know, yeah, yeah, yeah."

"Sorry, I just came here as I was passing, wasn't even sure if you'd be open."

"Yeah, yeah, yeah."

He grinned at me. I smiled weakly.

"Yeah, yeah, yeah," he said again, nodding and beaming. "Your T-shirt. The Beatles… Yeah, yeah, yeah."

"Ah, I see, yeah, yeah, yeah, The Beatles. I get it now."

I was a relieved man. I thought there was something wrong with him.

But the uncle working at the Memories of Old Ford Factory exhibition was as charming as he was considerate. He ushered me towards the start of the exhibition, pointing out the artifacts and offering his recommendations.

"Remember look up, look down, look all around," he said, as if teaching me to cross the road. "There are guns above your head and news clippings on the sides. Make sure you see everything and next time don't come so late, yeah, yeah, yeah."

I listened to his detailed instructions and then made my way towards what is perhaps the most significant room in the country's history. To a certain extent, today's Singapore was born in that room.

Cars have never particularly interested me, but the Ford Motor Company has somehow followed me through life. Its logo framed my childhood. As I walked up the Dagenham Heathway hill every morning to catch the Tube to secondary school, the belching chimneys of its factories along the River Thames filled the horizon line. From my mother to my wife's grandfather, everyone knew someone who had worked at Dagenham's Ford plant at some point. Ford defined Dagenham and Dagenham defined Ford; the two were interchangeable. My first published work, my university thesis, examined the impact of Ford's arrival on the Dagenham community. And after leaving Singapore – where Ford's first Southeast Asia assembly plant was set up in 1941 – I moved to Geelong, which happened to be the Ford town of Australia with its major assembly plant. But my deepest connection to Ford came from watching a 1970s British cop show called *The Sweeney,* where men with sublime sideburns and kipper ties drank too much, slept with lots of women and chased bank robbers across London's industrial estates in a Ford Granada or a Ford Cortina. In the darker recesses of my childlike mind,

I still believe that the secret to sleeping with lots of women is to own a classic Ford Cortina.

Of course, the Old Ford Motor Factory along Upper Bukit Timah Road also rubberstamped the greatest military disaster in British history, according to Churchill. It's already well known that Lieutenant-General Arthur Ernest Percival and General Tomoyuki Yamashita met in the Ford boardroom on 15th February 1942 and signed the surrender document, so I had wondered how engaging an exhibition built around a sparse, empty room might be. But the Surrender Chambers were chilling. The overactive air-conditioning didn't help, but the National Archives of Singapore, the site's custodian, had done a remarkable job in evoking a sense of time and place.

The exhibition was small, but compact and atmospheric. A short walk through a reconstructed tunnel, which provided audio-visual details of the Japanese invasion, led me to the Surrender Chambers. The minimalism was striking. The chairs were the actual chairs used in the Ford boardroom in 1942. The table was an exact replica and the clock on the wall was permanently set to 6.20pm; the moment Percival signed the document in that very room, the moment Singapore fell and the British Empire was exposed for what it really was. It's not oversimplifying to say that the world was never the same again after the brief, tense meeting in that room. Photos on the walls revealed how little the venue had actually changed. Alongside a timeline of events, the dialogue between the British and Japanese representatives was displayed on the panel outside. I found the experience deeply affecting.

The exhibition had some lovely touches and was a reminder that Singapore does this stuff really well, when it wants to, when it's allowed to. White fences from outside the old Parliament House had been used as installation art and an excellent map of Malaya incorporated glass from the old factory's green-tinted windows and tiles from its mosaic floors. As I listened to oral histories from Singaporean survivors of the Japanese occupation, I discovered two priceless, personal highlights of the exhibition gallery. First, I realised that the glass shield that bordered the interactive map of Malaya was actually a windscreen taken from a 1960s-built Ford Consul Cortina Mk II, the kind of car used in *The Sweeney*. And second, I read that the Ford Malaya plant assembled units in semi-knocked down conditions from its parent company back in... that's right... Dagenham.

"You little beauty!" I shouted.

It wasn't the wisest outburst as an interview with an elderly Singaporean discussing the hardships of the Japanese Occupation was playing at the time.

Still, an exhibition devoted to the single biggest event in Singapore's history, at the very location of the single biggest event in Singapore's history, had displayed a retro windscreen from a Ford Cortina and mentioned my hometown.

It truly made my day.

I was bounding towards the exit when my Beatles back-up singer called out to me. "Hey, you see everything in time?"

"Yep, it was terrific," I replied honestly.

"Hey, next time, don't come so late ah?"

He was still scolding me on the way out. I really liked him.

"No, I'll come earlier next time."

"Yeah, yeah, yeah," he cried, pointing at my Beatles T-shirt. "And you should tell lots of people about this place."

I couldn't agree more.

Memories at Old Ford Factory is the location where the Brits surrendered to the Japanese. And this is a windscreen from a classic Ford Cortina. So there are two important reasons to visit.

Beauty World's old shops and family businesses feel out of place in New Singapore. That's why they should be saved.

Fourteen

MY RELATIONSHIP with rats is straightforward. I am struck dumb by suriphobia, a fear of anything vaguely rodent. Those twitching whiskers, that swooshing tail. I'm terrified of the little furry fuckers.

But Singapore's relationship with rats is less straightforward. Where possible, we gloss over their existence. It's not a popular topic of conversation at the dinner table. I soon learned that genial hosts didn't appreciate it when I said: "Eh, you've got one hell of a rat eating his way through your void deck downstairs. I wasn't sure if it was a rat or a feeder bus. I thought about shooing him away. And then I thought about riding him home instead."

Rodents surround us all in Singapore, operating in the shadows, scavenging off our scraps, but no one wants to admit that the pests exist. A bit like loan sharks.

And then, the rats invaded Bukit Batok.

In December 2014, a frustrated resident recorded the rat infestation on the grassy slope beside Bukit Batok MRT station. There were hundreds of the blighters. There hadn't been a rat pack this audacious since Frank Sinatra hung out with the Vegas mafia. The resident witnessed more than 50 rats at the same site in 10 minutes and his clip went viral. Viral isn't good for the Singaporean powers that be. They're not overly keen on anything going viral beyond the Prime Minister in a funny hat on New Year's Eve. They'll tolerate the odd blogger selling formula milk or skincare products, but if they smell a rat online – let alone 50 of them – they send in the heavy mob. Or in this particular instance, they sent in the Star Pest Control firm. A spokesperson for the company told the press: "When we finish up the operation, we will eliminate the rats… we will just kill them." I defy anyone not to picture that spokesperson speaking with an Austrian accent and standing on the Bukit Batok summit with a bazooka on his shoulder.

But the situation called for the T-100 of the rat terminating business, with the cold, rational voice of a trained killing machine. All else was chaos. The residents blamed the "Gahmen", naturally. Since the explosion of social media, those "Gahmen" guys have been blamed for everything from HDB flat prices to the price of oil, climate change, the shortage of Hello Kitty dolls and kids not clearing their trays away at hawker centres. But the "Gahmen" is a fragmented beast, making shameless blame-shifting more entertaining than a naked game of pass the sausage. SMRT controlled the adjacent station and its growing number of food outlets (despite early warnings from the London Underground that food on an urban, subterranean rail network attracts cable-chomping, disease-carrying rodents). But it wasn't SMRT's fault. NParks managed the nearby Bukit Batok Park, which presumably offered a five-star suite of accommodation options for the little burrowers. But it wasn't their fault. HDB managed the state land on which the grassy slope was situated, but it wasn't their fault. The town council oversaw the cleaning and maintenance of the entire Bukit Batok estate. Surprisingly, it wasn't their fault. So, the country kicked the dog. The finger of blame was pointed towards a few, malnourished stray dogs.

The rat infestation wasn't the result of food establishments mushrooming around the MRT station, or the proliferation of overflowing dustbins along the walkway, or our physical inability to take one giant leap for Mankind all the way to the tray return area. According to the authorities, it was those animal welfare do-gooders feeding the strays. They had been told time and again to leave the dogs alone, but they selfishly insisted on helping the less fortunate in the community. Letter writers asked the governing powers to consider the usual course of action in such circumstances. Kill them. Kill them all. (I'm referring to the stray dogs, not the stray dog feeders. We love a culling programme, but not of people. The paperwork would be a bureaucratic nightmare.)

Of course, the SPCA pointed out that a core group of designated community feeders left small amounts of food at specific areas for the dogs and, unlike many of the human folks eating at the coffee shops nearby, they cleaned up after themselves. So a consensus of right-minded citizens decided it was probably for the best if the dogs were spared. But the rats had no chance. The pest controllers marched to the top of the hill and by the time they marched down again for the last time, they took 300 dead rats with them.

During the three-week operation, however, Singaporeans seemed to talk about nothing else. A taboo subject was being openly discussed, along with a number of other, equally pertinent concerns. Why are we so quick to shift blame to others? Why do we leave our parks and gardens like an explosion in a paint factory after public events? Why can't we clean up after ourselves? Why do we act like those tray return counters are coated with gelignite?

The rats of Bukit Batok forced Singapore to address some difficult questions about its proud food culture and the traditional notion that abundance should be celebrated, rather than reined in. The rats got us talking about rats and our culinary and hygiene habits, not to mention our indolence at hawker centres.

But the town's reputation suffered.

When I told a neighbour I was off to Bukit Batok, he said: "Wah, you the Pied Piper, is it? You want to visit rats?"

"Er, yeah."

But I never found any. I wandered up and down the grassy slope beside the MRT station, picking out the handiwork of the pest controllers, some nets around deserted burrows, but no rodents.

"Excuse me, I've got a strange question," I asked a guy removing a padlock on his bicycle at the MRT station racks. "Have you seen any rats?"

"Where? Where?" He jumped back and looked around his feet.

"No, no, not here, over there at the grassy slope, that's where they were before, right?"

"Don't know. Never saw."

I stopped asking people after a few more rejections. I was freaking them out. So I headed off to correct a couple of wrongs instead.

The rat hysteria had left Bukit Batok with an underserved stigma. The attractive estate, practically surrounded by parks and forest, was an established, quiet community that had found itself pushed into the limelight by a voracious rodent colony. And, more embarrassingly, I had never featured Bukit Batok in my previous Singapore books, a fact often pointed out to me by Bukit Batok residents. They usually championed Little Guilin Park. I usually agreed that it was one of Singapore's finest parks.

I'd never been there.

So I got back on the train, travelled one stop to Bukit Gombak, made my way through a sizeable crowd of joggers at the nearby stadium, surely a contender for Singapore's most agreeable sports venue with the lush hilly terrain behind its running track, and then clambered down a stone staircase into Bukit Batok Town Park. To many, it's known as Little Guilin. To me, it's just about perfect.

The place won me over immediately. A short slope led me to the water's edge and its stunning, sweeping vista. I was greeted by that imposing granite cliff face, twice as commanding with its silhouette reflected in the calm, still lake waters. Dense forest surrounded the lake on either side of the granite rock, giving the appearance of a elongated, green-bearded face with a bulbous nose, if you tilted your face until it was horizontal (as I did, much to the amusement of a couple of Filipinos snogging on a bench. They only came up for air to giggle at me before going back to eating each other). Little Guilin – Xiao Guilin – gets its name from Guilin in China, where there is a similar granite rock by a lake.

And, like so many other features of Old Singapore, one should be grateful that it's still here. In the 1980s, HDB had considered filling in the disused granite quarry to build a road across it. Fortunately common sense prevailed (and an element of economic wisdom no doubt – Little Guilin was surrounded by condos battling each other for the best view of its green hills).

For years, the rugged rocks above the lake have framed many Singaporean wedding photos and its romantic setting remains a draw for amorous couples. I left the frolicking Filipinos fondling each other on the bench and practically fell into a young Indian woman straddling her man inside a concrete shelter. I'd stepped inside to take out a drink and almost sat on top of them. They had clothes on, of course, but I somehow felt seedy and grubby. I probably shouldn't have asked to record a short video for an online "news" site. (I'm kidding. I didn't have much left on the phone battery.) But they didn't look up. Not once. She just gyrated slightly and he moaned a little; it was that faint, masculine moan that I only produce these days when my running daughter accidentally head butts me in the groin. But I recognised that the pair wanted to be left alone. So I put my binoculars away and walked out.

Besieged by courting couples, I felt lonely in such a romantic setting. I decided to leave.

"Hey, I like you," a voice said in the encroaching darkness.

Perhaps my luck was changing.

"I thought it was you. Yeah, I really like you."

It was a male voice. The trip to Little Guilin was proving to be a night of firsts.

"Yeah, yeah, Humphreys, right?"

A handsome middle-aged Chinese guy dressed in luminous running gear stepped into the streetlight.

"Er, yes, it's me," I replied cautiously.

"Yah, I thought so," he beamed, almost as brightly as his yellow running outfit. "I been reading your books for years."

The anti-climax was crushing. He noticed my notepad.

"You doing a book now? About Bukit Batok?" he asked enthusiastically, one of life's genuinely kind souls.

"Er, well, sort of, I'm just picking out some of Singapore's, you know, old stuff, rarer stuff, like Little Guilin here, like Old Singapore, its older gems," I stammered, as if explaining a vintage range of jewellery.

"Then you must go to the Bukit Batok Nature Park!" he exclaimed.

"I thought this was it."

"No, this is the town park, the nature park on the east side."

It was already dark. My withering feet were threatening a walkout.

"I'm really tired," I admitted. "How far is it?"

"Ah, it's only about 10 minutes," he said, eyeing my gangly frame. "For you, maybe 15 minutes."

"I can do it in 10 minutes. Ten minutes is no problem."

SECONDS LATER, I found myself hurtling along Bukit Batok East Avenue 5 in defiance of my long, creaking limbs. I ignored the tweaked hamstring that had begun the day throbbing but now screamed like Miley Cyrus on a wrecking ball, and petulantly threw myself down Bukit Batok East Avenue 2. I followed the Hillview park connector and turned into a pitch-black park I'd never really heard of.

There were people everywhere. They kept appearing through the shadows and from behind trees and toilet blocks. It was like *The Walking Dead*. Families, joggers, cyclists, buggy walkers, skating buggers, hand-holders and tree huggers had all congregated for a moonlight stroll, getting together at car parks and meeting points and greeting one another like masons rolling up a trouser leg at private initiation rituals. It was such an uplifting scene, Singaporeans gathering on a Friday night to savour nothing but stillness. At the pond, one couple had a feel for each other. They didn't appreciate the accidental intrusion. In Bukit Batok, I seemed to be a physical form of coitus interruptus.

But Bukit Batok Nature Park had the lot: walking trails, another fine lake in a rugged quarry (abandoned in 1988), children's playgrounds, splendid views and a World War II heritage site (a memorial for Japanese soldiers). Between the Nature Park and Lake Guilin, Bukit Batok is blessed with more green space than most housing estates in Singapore (and the Bukit Timah Nature Reserve is just across from Bukit Batok Nature Park). Being on the *ulu* side of Singapore, the town doesn't seem to capture national attention quite as often as the central communities of, say, Ang Mo Kio, Toa Payoh or Queenstown, and I've been guilty of neglecting the western estates in the past. I won't again.

I was on the phone to my wife, telling her as much, when Batman flew overhead.

Instinctively, I ducked.

"Bloody hell, I'll call you back… Did you see that?"

Pocketing my phone, I turned towards a couple of Indian guys sitting at a nearby table, still in their dusty work clothes.

One of them eyed me warily.

"What?"

"There, up there, look, flew over my head, it's huge."

His eyes widened.

"Oh yah… Come."

He beckoned his friend and they both joined me: two Indians and an *ang moh*, open-mouthed and staring at the tree trunk in front of us.

With effortless grace, a colugo had glided over my head and landed on the tree. Seconds later, a second swooped in and joined its pal. The three of us whooped like kids watching a fireworks display for the first time. I hadn't seen a colugo in the wild before, let alone two treating my head like a homing beacon along their flight path.

"Amazing," I muttered to my companions. "I've never seen them in the wild."

"Me also," replied the guy standing beside me. "What is it?"

"It's a colugo, like a flying fox, you know the ones that kind of look like squirrels stuck to a hang glider and go like this."

Caught up in the moment – I do love a wild encounter in a natural environment – I stretched out my arms and proceeded to circle the two Indian chaps in a gliding motion that wasn't so much the Dark Knight as it was white pillock.

"Oh a bat, a bat," the talkative one said, perhaps eager for the tall stranger to stop encircling him in a moonlit forest.

"No, not a bat, this is a colugo, it doesn't fly, it glides, much bigger, see."

He took a step back. "Does it bite?"

"Bite?"

"Yah, like… argh." He snarled and bit into the air, channelling his best Dracula.

"You mean, like a vampire?"

"Yah, yah."

"No."

"Oh."

Relieved that they were not extras in a *Twilight* movie, the brave duo stepped forward again. Right on cue, a third colugo soared overhead and dropped down on a second tree trunk. We were awestruck, rooted to the spot as our fellow mammals foraged for food. Three colugos, two Indians and an *ang moh* shared a moment together inside a breezy forest canopy, beneath a cloudless sky. I felt like hugging my new friends. But I had probably scared them enough.

Little Guilin Park could be the answer to Singapore's baby-making problems. People can't keep their hands off each other inside the shelters.

Go to Bukit Batok Nature Park during the day for the view. Go at night for the colugos.

Fifteen

SINGAPORE'S PRIME MINISTER Lee Hsien Loong made the unexpected revelation on live TV in 2014. The Mandai area, already home to the Singapore Zoo, the Night Safari and the River Safari, had been earmarked for radical redevelopment. And the iconic Jurong Bird Park, according to the Prime Minister, could be relocated to Mandai. Well, the public shock was palpable. In a rare moment of solidarity, the entire country appeared to stand as one to ask the same question of its government.

Is the Jurong Bird Park still open?

Ah, the Jurong Bird Park. The perception of one of Singapore's oldest attractions is like that of an eccentric relative; much cherished, but a little out of touch and always followed by a faint whiff of bird droppings. For many, Jurong Bird Park is the boring bit of a modern, trendy zoo that visitors pass quickly to get to the lions and tigers and bears. It's essentially a collection of birds. Now I love birds as much as the next Hitchcock horror fan, but in the animal food chain of modern tourism, the feathered flappers come a distant second to the big cats and great apes, like a canapé before the fillet steak.

So I had low expectations ahead of our family day out to the Jurong Bird Park. My wife and I had visited in 1997 and had vague memories of the place (there were lots of birds), but our daughter struggled with the concept as we travelled along the expressway.

"Can we see the hippopotamus?" she asked.

"No, it's a bird park," I reminded her. "It's just birds."

"Oh, yeah, I like penguins. Penguins are cute."

"Good."

"But we can see the monkeys, Daddy, right?"

The Ayer Rajah Expressway had never seemed longer. And nor had the queue outside the Jurong Bird Park. I anticipated a fading, tired tourist attraction, somewhere between Haw Par Villa's death throes and the perseverance of Fort Siloso, which refuses to succumb to market forces despite the obvious public indifference. I was certain that was going to be Jurong Bird Park, just a few coach parties from China and India, a handful of backpackers looking for a cheaper day out before returning to Serangoon Road, a few old aviaries, bored penguins behind glass and a lame show involving a parrot singing *Polly, Put the Kettle On*.

I couldn't have been more wrong.

Crowds jostled for space at the ticket counter. Despite being a wannabe ornithologist with a fine pair of binoculars, even I found myself saying to my wife: "It's still just birds, right? Why is this place so popular? Have they added a rare carnivorous bird that eats foreigners?"

Jurong Bird Park was built and popularised in a world that predated social media, the Internet, VHS and colour TV in Singapore. With extraordinary – and often overlooked – foresight, Goh Keng Swee visited the free-flight aviary at the Rio zoo in 1968 and thought that Singapore should build something similar. The Minister of Finance decided that Jurong's mushrooming industrial zone needed greening up a bit and dropped the world's largest bird zoo between the grey factories just three years later. Goh's vision would still be considered remarkable today, let alone in 1971 when much of Singapore was still swampy and undeveloped. No one examines the master plan of a fledgling industrial estate in the late '60s and calls for a flock of pretty flamingos without the help of LSD.

But Goh had. His idea was spectacularly realised and people were still coming to visit. Making our way through the throng was particularly problematic as my wife had broken a bone in her foot and was forced to wear one of those medical moonboots that reduced her walk to a slow limp and suggested she was going to take a leap for Mankind at any moment. Holding her by the elbow, I eased her through the ticket barrier. A Jurong Bird Park employee bounded over.

"Hey, madam, you've hurt your foot," he said.

"Nothing gets past you, does it?"

My wife elbowed me in the ribs.

"Come, I'll help you."

And he returned with a wheelchair, free of charge. I thought about kissing him. An hour later, I thought about killing my wife. The park was built on the edge of Jurong Hill and came with almost as many steep inclines as it did birds.

I won't list all the attractions– you've all been here at some point – but the Lory Loft, the Flamingo Lake and the African Waterfall Aviary had retained their appeal. Jurong Falls still impressed. In the World of Darkness, which showcased the nocturnal birds, I encountered my favourite mammal tapping the exhibit's glass with a selfie stick. Using a system of reverse lighting, the birdhouse played God a bit, turning night into day and vice versa, and the dim conditions were allowing the Addams Family to test the high-powered intensity of their camera flashes. I had tried to ignore the inanity of their conversation as I followed them through the birdhouse, whilst holding onto a wary daughter and pushing my wife's wheelchair. We waited behind them at the owl enclosure as the father tapped the glass, just above the sign reminding visitors not to touch the glass.

"Look, look," said the excited father. "The owl's looking at me!"

Well, of course he is, mate. You've just whacked his window with a selfie stick.

I stepped towards him and felt my wife's hand on my arm. Wives read minds. I pulled back. We neared the end of the World of Darkness and caught up with the Addams' in front of the buffy fish owl. Mummy held the baby and tapped the window with the selfie stick as Daddy unleashed a flash bright enough to drown out the stars over Jurong Island. The owl craned its head, its traumatised eyes glaring at the family.

"Ah see, see, it's looking. OK, tap again," said fidgety Daddy holding his long-lensed camera. "OK, look here, look here, ready, one, two three!... OK, that one blurred. Tap the window again, ready..."

"OK, what are you doing," I said.

Everyone was suddenly looking at me – even the owl.

"Taking a photo," the Daddy said.

"But it says quite clearly no tapping and no flash photography. Are you really this blur or are you doing an impression?"

We ended our brief encounter there. The family turned their backs to me and made for the exit. And, in my flash of anger, I had turned my back on my wife and her wheelchair was disappearing down the slope.

Still, the Addams Family couldn't spoil our trip to the Jurong Bird Park. But a few state planners might. New Singapore's steely-eyed focus could be less hardheaded on this one. Logic dictates that a tourist attraction left behind in the industrial heartland may not be sustainable in the long-term. But if the bird park moves to Mandai, then Goh's vision back in 1968 is at risk of becoming the boring bit of a wildlife banquet, an appetiser easily skipped by tourists on stopovers or tight schedules (and Singaporeans, for that matter).

Of course, there is also the chance that the bird park will find itself left behind by its bigger, brash Mandai siblings if it remains in Jurong. But it stands alone, like Regent's Park Zoo and Central Park Zoo, both of which could presumably be moved to more expansive locations. But their iconic status derives partially from their name and location. The counter argument of an unappealing, remote location cannot apply in tiny Singapore and, in any case, such a suggestion infers an elitist approach, i.e. build everything around Marina Bay or Bukit Timah and let the far-flung estates of Jurong come to us. Can the established communities not be permitted to keep what they already have? No one has had any trouble finding the park in the last 40-odd years. For generations of Singaporeans, it's always been the Jurong Bird Park, a genuine original. The park's innovative backstory doesn't warrant a damp squib for a postscript, where a pioneering icon becomes an optional extra at the Mandai animal emporium. Like the buffy fish owl, the Jurong Bird Park really should be left alone.

NOW, MY WIFE has a proper job. She rises early, packs a bag and grabs our daughter and they both head off to school as teacher and student respectively. In theory, I get up when I want and strut around Singapore with a notepad desperately trying to convince the voices in my head – all of which sound disturbingly like my wife – that my career constitutes real work. Working-class guilt continues to haunt me. I was denied the kind of affluent upbringing that considers, say, organising dinner parties a socially acceptable occupation. (And why, incidentally, do I keep meeting these people in New Singapore?

Is there a shortage of corporate party planners? Who did we hire before? Ronald McDonald?) My family all had real, labour-intensive jobs, like building houses, driving buses or working with special needs children. Writing was something you did on postcards whilst shivering on a British beach.

My lingering, nagging guilt, buried deep within that stubborn chip on the shoulder, was excavated by my full-time teaching, full-time mothering wife.

"So where are you off to today?" she asked, as she chased our Hi-5-dancing daughter around the living room.

"Choa Chu Kang," I mumbled.

"What's Choa Chu Kang got from Old Singapore?" she enquired, whilst informing our daughter that there wasn't time before school to do a robot dance.

"Bus stops," I whispered.

My wife stopped. My daughter continued her robot dancing.

"You're going all the way to Choa Chu Kang to see some bus stops?"

"No, no, just the one bus stop."

I'm sure she ponders divorce in such moments.

"I'm looking after our daughter before and after school so you can see a bus stop?" she asked.

"It's not just a bus stop, it's the oldest bus stop in Singapore and has real cultural significance and, don't forget, we met at a bus stop and… "

"We met at a bowling alley."

"All right, Columbo, do you have to remember everything?"

"I've got to go to work," my wife said.

"I'm a robot," my daughter said.

I was left alone in the living room.

It wasn't so much the bus stop that concerned my wife, as it was my obvious eagerness to track down the bus stop. It's not exactly an aphrodisiac. Women rarely show an interest in men with a soft spot for retro bus stops. But I was excited to find the preserved bus stops of Choa Chu Kang, in particular the one that was Singapore's first. They are rare beneficiaries of people power (within clearly defined boundaries, of course).

In 2008, a Land Transport Authority survey was published in *The Straits Times* calling upon readers to pick local landmarks and heritage sites that might be potentially saved. Choa Chu Kang's concrete bus stops, built in the 1970s and the only ones of their kind left, received the highest number of votes. Now I realise that it's easy to be cynical. Even at the time, the survey smacked of tokenism. Options were largely limited to areas and locations that made their preservation relatively painless. Saving bus stops in Singapore's largely undisturbed military zone hardly equated to sparing Bukit Brown Cemetery.

But the public plumped for the bus stops nonetheless. Singapore's dependence upon public transport gives all of us a literal and spiritual connection to them. We all take buses. We all sit at bus stops to go to school, to work, to play, to eat, to hold hands with our partners or steal a final kiss from the kids. We all identify. It's no coincidence that of all the online lists and blogs that reminisce about Old Singapore, the photos of old buses and trains often trigger the most comments and memories. It's an immediate nostalgic kneejerk, a sudden reconnection to a lost past. We all hailed those taxis. We all took those buses. Those photos, just like the Choa Chu Kang bus stops, unite us in our sentimentality in a country that has for so long seen sentimentality as some sort of weakness. Sentimentality serves little purpose in a growing economy. It's just an old bus stop. It doesn't put food on the table. Why should anyone care?

But people do. Or at least, enough to win the bus stops a reprieve. Perhaps Singapore's endless evolution into something bigger, faster, grander and more foreign has inadvertently forced residents to look back towards something smaller, slower, simpler and local. It can be disorienting to not recognise one's home. They might only be bus stops, but at least they were clearly and obviously Singaporean bus stops.

And Singaporeans, damn it, decided to take their bus stops back.

But I'm glad I didn't take my wife. After spending the best part of two hours on trains and buses, I spotted Singapore's oldest bus stop through the bus window as we trundled along Old Choa Chu Kang Road. I felt a sudden surge of adrenaline. I know, I know. It's a bus stop. But it's not so much the landmark as it is the thrill of the hunt and the subsequent discovery. I've visited the temples of Luxor and stood atop the Empire State Building and climbed the Sydney Harbour Bridge, but I was no less excited when I stumbled upon Cashin House in the Lim Chu Kang mangroves, or a single rotten timber beam that had once held up an old Dagenham railway bridge in the 1930s – or the concrete bus stop opposite the Tengah Air Base.

Its heritage jumped out at me as I stepped off the No. 975. The bus stop wasn't particularly practical. Made of concrete, the long shelter was held up by seven pillars that were neatly decorated with an ornate, curved orange railing, but offered little protection from the elements. The absence of a glass wall or shield ensured the bus stop provided an unblocked, breezy view of the Tengah forest behind, but probably didn't keep out the rain. Still, the concrete bench was cooler than those plastic seats that are no doubt cheaper, but come with a free thigh waxing.

A plaque or an informational panel might improve the quirky piece of island heritage further, but I was certainly glad I visited. As I took some photos, I noticed a military man in a bluish uniform with an air of importance that suggested he was a superior rank (that's the extent of my military knowledge). He stepped back to avoid being caught on camera.

"It's OK, I'm just taking a photo of the bus stop. I'm not a weirdo or anything," I gabbled, sounding exactly like a weirdo taking photos of an empty bus stop.

He nodded and returned to playing with his phone.

"I don't usually take photos of bus stops in remote areas, it's just that this bus stop is quite historic," I blathered on.

He smiled warily, like you do at that guy who suddenly starts singing on a bus.

Fortunately, five younger, jokey uniformed guys from Tengah Air Base joined us. Their appearance was intimidating: all camouflaged fatigues, shiny boots and bulked up physiques from NS training. They weren't quite *An Officer and a Gentleman,* more an Officer and an Ah Beng, but they looked the part. Relaxed by their safety in numbers, they stretched out across the heritage bus stop and made the usual crude jokes, until one showed off his portable speaker.

"Hey, I don't bluff you OK," he said. "This one damn good, listen."

As he switched on the device, I expected Kanye West or Jay-Z. I certainly didn't anticipate Richard Marx. That caught me off guard. I always think a Richard Marx ballad is missing something, usually a sick bucket. So I really didn't expect Ah Boy to start singing the bloody thing. Closing his eyes, the military man held the speaker and crooned: "Wherever you go, whatever you do, I will be right here waiting for you."

You don't often see hardened soldiers singing power ballads at bus stops. The visuals just didn't match the torturous audio, like watching Schwarzenegger sing *The Sound of Music.* National servicemen may be trained in the dark arts of interrogation to extract information, but I draw the line at using Richard Marx.

Jurong Falls at the Jurong Bird Park is a quintessentially Singaporean view. It's man-made and entirely artificial.

I spent two hours on public transport to visit Singapore's oldest bus stop in Old Choa Chu Kang Road. My wife didn't understand either.

Sixteen

THE BUS DRIVER kept glancing up at me through his rear-view mirror. I was the only passenger left on his bus as we sped along Lim Chu Kang Road. As we passed Sungei Gedong Road, I pressed the bell. He looked puzzled.

"You sure ah," he shouted down the empty bus. "This one ah?"

"Yeah, this bus stop, thanks."

"There's nothing here, you know."

"It's all right, I know where I'm going."

"OK, take care ah."

I understood his concern. I was nowhere, left alone in the northwestern corner of Singapore. Remote forest surrounded me. There were no cars or people, just the quiet, consistent hum of chirping insects. I crossed Lim Chu Kang Road to face an abandoned housing estate, an estate that some Singaporeans believe to be haunted and refuse to visit. The crumbling, rotting Neo Tiew area is one of the creepiest landmarks Old Singapore has to offer.

In the first of many unusual oddities, the estate takes its name from a sheriff. Neo Tiew, a Chinese immigrant, founded Lim Chu Kang village, established a school and a clinic and ended up being sheriff of Singapore's northern frontier. He also assisted the British in the defence of Lim Chu Kang and Changi during the Japanese invasion. He ended up with a road and the island's strangest housing estate named after him. The Neo Tiew Estate was a horror movie set waiting for a shooting script. Even in the day, the place was unnerving, partly because it was crawling with green men armed with machine guns. The Neo Tiew compound had been taken over for a military drill. Being so close to the Sungei Gedong camp, it's a ready-made location to play "halt, who goes there" in the empty units and corridors.

I stopped by the fence that bordered the empty flats and immediately ruled out trespassing. Ordinarily, I'd have a go. For a recent Singaporean TV documentary, I strayed into an empty black and white bungalow and was improvising a riveting piece to camera when I was promptly arrested. Well, I wasn't so much arrested as I was held temporarily by a couple of young, wildly enthusiastic police officers not entirely convinced by my story.

"We are just filming a documentary about some of Singapore's greatest properties," I said truthfully. "And I wasn't sure if this place was off limits."

"There are trespassing signs everywhere," a junior policeman pointed out.

"Ah, we didn't really see them and thought the property was open to the public."

"Your cameraman climbed in through the window."

"Did he? I didn't know that."

"You gave him a leg up to help him through the window. We saw you on CCTV."

In the end, our identity cards were confiscated and we were threatened with a trespassing charge unless we deleted all the video footage of the property in their presence, which was more than fair. But I had wasted an entire day's filming. So the moral of that particular story, kids, is never, under any circumstances, trespass in Singapore. Ever.

Unless you're absolutely sure there are no CCTV cameras.

So I heeded the warnings around the Neo Tiew Estate. I followed the racist no-trespassing signs. No, they're not really racist, but they always depict a camouflaged soldier shooting a white man. Who are they shooting, Anton Casey? I wandered around the edges of the estate, peering through the fence, taking the odd photo and generally minimising my chances of getting shot. The spookiness was inescapable. Kampong Silat was also abandoned, but the Singapore Investment Trust built those flats. HDB designed Neo Tiew. It was an eerie, empty HDB estate in the middle of a forest. The mind struggled with the mismatched images. And the children's playground was something else. Obviously one of the oldest in Singapore, the kiddie corner had a Victorian carousel-styled rocking horse, a seesaw straight from the 1970s and a slide and climbing frame being strangled by weeds. It was a playground from the village of the damned, only missing a one-eyed zombie kid with long, flowing hair drifting past and singing *Ring o Ring o Roses*.

What made Neo Tiew particularly fascinating were its obvious, identifiable features. Built in 1979, the compound still had everything in place; the three-storey flats, the wet market and hawker centre, the playground and the void decks and their stone tables and benches. Everything was there except the people, a community missing its community. The decaying, peeling nature of the desolate estate reminded me of Hashima Island in Japan. The former coal-mining facility was abandoned when petrol replaced coal in the 1960s and the housing complex was left behind. In recent years, the island's surreal ruins have gained international interest after the concrete buildings were featured in both the documentary *Life After People* and the James Bond movie *Skyfall*. I found Neo Tiew no less fascinating. When it went en-bloc and its residents moved out in 2002, the area immediately became an above-ground time capsule of an early HDB community.

Neo Tiew should really be open to Singaporeans beyond those with green-painted faces (unlikely, I know, as the estate is mostly used by the military for the wonderful acronym FIBUA – fighting in built-up areas).

Unfortunately, the graffiti was less interesting. The estate has some exceptional street art within the compound, according to previous visitors/trespassers, but I couldn't validate their claim, as I was the only person in the area without a gun. The only graffiti I spotted, scrawled on corridors and void decks, was the word "fuck". The scribble seemed like a wasted opportunity. The end hadn't justified the exhausting means. The vandals had already done the hard part. They'd grabbed their marker pens and scaled the fence under the cover of darkness, only to turn into a couple of Tourette's sufferers once faced with a large white wall.

"Quick, what shall we write?"

"Fuck!"

"OK, set. What else shall we write?"

"Fuck!"

"Done. What else? Don't tell me, let me guess."

"Fuck!"

"Exactly."

The Neo Tiew Estate deserves a better class of criminal.

I IMPROVISED when I left Lim Chu Kang. Reading the map, I realised I was reasonably close to the ACRES Wildlife Rescue Centre and decided to pay the animal sanctuary an unscheduled visit. I had to see a man about a dolphin.

Two years earlier, I had contacted ACRES founder Louis Ng with an unusual request.

"Hello, Louis," I wrote on Facebook. "I need a dolphin."

"Yeah, I can get you a dolphin," he replied in my message box. "How many you need?"

"Oh, one will be enough."

"You sure? I can get you two if you need them."

We settled on a single dolphin. And one Saturday afternoon, Louis staggered through the Forum shopping mall, perspiring heavily and carrying a life-size plastic dolphin. Kids followed him. Parents wondered if he was organising a photo session with a cartoon character. The marine mammal featured in a children's book I had written and I figured a life-sized dolphin, mounted on a stand in an arching, balletic pose, might impress the children at the book launch. It certainly did. One or two livelier boys clambered onto the stage and unwittingly tried to mount the dolphin by grabbing its undercarriage. I had to interrupt my storytelling to free Willy.

The rise and rise of ACRES (or the Animal Concerns Research & Education Society Singapore) is such a feel-good story, it should come with a Richard Marx soundtrack. Founded by Louis in 2001, the non-profit organisation now has 18,000 supporters and volunteers and tackles that paradox between old and new Singapore. The charity works to preserve what's left of the indigenous residents across the island, thanks to a committed band of activists striving to change established cultural habits. In other words, Old Singapore's wildlife can only be saved if some of Old Singapore's lifestyle choices are dropped. If you want the sharks, give up the shark's fin soup. If you want the pangolin, give up the habitat destruction, that sort of thing.

And to muddy the waters further, it's increasingly younger Singaporeans telling older Singaporeans where they're going wrong in life. No one likes a smart arse, particularly when the gentle chiding involves eating choices. Singaporeans will just about tolerate snarling traffic, ERP prices and packed MRT trains, but don't think about messing with their food.

In some ways, I envy previous generations. There was a degree of awareness when it came to climate change, the planet's depleted resources and the mistreatment of all species, but ignorance still largely reigned. They chopped down trees, shot anything that survived, built homes smothered in asbestos, boiled bowls of shark's fin soup, washed that down with pints of black bear's bile and spent holidays whooping as confused dolphins jumped through hula-hoops to earn a dead fish. It was a mostly guilt-free existence and they'd be damned if a smarmy kid in an ACRES T-shirt at a shopping mall roadshow was going to point out the error of their ways.

This is what ACRES is up against. The war rages on, but the charity is winning battles. In 2009, its rescue centre opened. Volunteers conduct wildlife awareness programmes at schools and workplaces. They have established clear government ties and, more impressively, ACRES is now a reputable brand name and a go-to organisation for animal welfare. Most Singaporeans know whom to call and this wasn't always the case. In the late '90s, my wife and I came across an escaped rabbit on a Bishan void deck. For an hour, we chased that floppy-eared bugger like deranged magicians. Eventually, we cornered Thumper and called the police. They thanked us for our selfless efforts and said the owner might come forward to collect the lost pet. He didn't. The rabbit was put down the following day.

The walk along the serene Jalan Lekar was much further than I had anticipated. By the time I dragged my melting, leaking frame past the eye-catching mural on the side of the rescue centre, I was ready to drop. And I hadn't made an appointment.

"This is our lunch hour, there's no one around," said a polite young woman. "We can't take visitors around the rescue centre without an appointment."

"But I was nearby and I've walked a long way," I pleaded.

"Yah, you do look sweaty. OK, come."

Her name was Sharrel and she was just lovely. She gave up her lunch hour to play tour guide, pointing out the rescued reptile enclosure. A Great Asian horn turtle meandered past my feet. Its shell had been glued back together after being hit by a truck. There were recovering star tortoises and an enormous African Spurred tortoise, all victims of poaching. The charity was only licensed to take in reptiles – all other animals get referred to the zoo – but was in the process of applying for a licence to provide shelters for other animals. In Singapore, everything needs a licence.

Sharrel led me into the indoor classroom, where volunteers give presentations on conservation, and I came across my old friend.

"Hey, it's my dolphin," I exclaimed, stroking the plastic model on its head. "Louis let me borrow this one."

"Yeah, we used this for our roadshows," Sharrel said. "Did Louis use the manacles and the tears on the dolphin's face?"

"No, no, it was a children's book launch."

The dolphin was ordinarily used to promote awareness of the ongoing farce at Resorts World Sentosa's Marine Life Park. At the time of my visit to ACRES, four wild-caught bottlenose dolphins had already died at the tourist attraction. ACRES had compiled a petition with more than 100,000 signatures demanding the rehabilitation and release of the dolphins back into the ocean. But Resorts World Sentosa insisted that the remaining 23 dolphins were healthy and the attraction increased public awareness of marine biodiversity. Obviously, the best way to promote the precarious life of marine mammals is to haul in two-dozen wild dolphins from the ocean and offer them as photo opportunities for tour parties as a means of killing time before they return to the blackjack. Bottle-nose dolphins are extraordinarily intelligent mammals and can reach swimming speeds of up to 30km per hour. They are not designed for a life in captivity. On the plus side, their view of Keppel Harbour is said to be lovely.

But the 14 full-time staff at ACRES – along with the 60 volunteers they get every month – are doing their bit. In fact, they are doing so much more, something quite profound. They are calling on the best of New Singapore (younger, committed, compassionate animal welfare campaigners) to save the best of Old Singapore (the island's native wildlife and what remains of its natural habitat). It's not a bad template to follow.

I thanked Sharrel for the unexpected tour and gave my plastic friend a final pat on the head, wallowing in my moral superiority. Like Resorts World Sentosa, I once borrowed a dolphin that didn't belong to me. But I sent my one back.

It feels like the end of the world at the remote, abandoned Neo Tiew Estate. And for me it almost was with all those soldiers with machine guns.

ACRES Wildlife Rescue Centre saves the vulnerable residents of Old Singapore. It also does a nice line in plastic dolphin loans.

Seventeen

ANIMAL ENCOUNTERS usually say more about us than the animal. We react in entirely different ways. In 2012, a young boy was knocked over by a charging wild boar at Bishan-Ang Mo Kio Park. The boar had run in from the encroaching forest of Lower Pierce Reservoir, dashed across the playground and sent the poor kid – who wasn't seriously injured – tumbling. No parent expects a child to be pushed over by a wild boar at the local park (although when I was a kid, I did own a dog that occasionally peed on peoples' legs at parks). But the reaction to the rare attack was mostly balanced and informed. There was a general consensus that we had to share the island. NParks would have to monitor and control the population of wild boars who, let's face it, do like to shag and produce lots of little piglets. And that was that. We moved on with our lives.

But there's always one. There's always going to be one or two stern letter writers to the media who probably shouldn't be left home alone with a laptop. They tolerate nothing and no one. They struggle to see beyond the self. They usually drive faster to prevent another vehicle from pulling into their lane or closer to intimidate a cyclist. They refuse to give up their seats on trains and buses. They complain when property prices are too high and they cannot buy, or too low and they cannot sell. They moan that there are too many foreigners in the country, squeezing their profit margins; or not enough foreigners in the country, forcing them to pay higher salaries to Singaporeans and squeezing their profit margins. They criticise the Government for turning the country into an omnipresent nanny state that removes all sense of self-responsibility and personal autonomy, then hand their homes and children over to foreign helpers. They expect a litter-free existence, demanding that any unwanted, unhelpful or unappealing obstacle be instantly removed from their sanitised path through life. Whether it's a rat, cat, dog, wild boar, monkey or snake, they want them caught, castrated and culled immediately. Or they're going to write a stern letter to the media.

You know. Those people.

Fortunately, they are being challenged at every turn. Farsighted folks are keeping an eye on the future by protecting the past. They're not building an Ark, growing beards and singing *Kumbaya*, but they are establishing greener gateways and challenging individuals to recognise the existence of others a bit more. Sungei Buloh Nature Reserve continues to lead the way in this regard. The coastal forest not only represents Old Singapore, but the mangrove also provides the island's oldest residents with a genuinely safe haven. There aren't many left.

And that brings us back to animal encounters and how our instinctive reactions reveal so much about us.

I saw a wild crocodile.

Other Sungei Buloh visitors also saw the crocodile.

We didn't shout, scream, run or reach for a phone or a gun. Nor did we dash off a letter to the newspaper forum pages demanding the immediate extermination of all native estuarine crocodiles between here and Selangor, calling for a cross-Causeway agreement to hunt down anything predatory and reptilian (I'm still talking about crocodiles, not dodgy staff at Sim Lim Square). Instead, we gathered on the boardwalk, respectfully and sensibly to admire a creature that has been stalking these swamps since the days of dinosaurs.

Sungei Buloh was already home to Singapore's largest mangrove forest (130 hectares, or 130 football fields) before its 31-hectare extension was opened to the public in December 2014. From Kranji MRT Station, I had taken the No. 975 to the Kranji Way car park to visit the expanded reserve. Every aspect impressed. A new entrance at Kranji Way, opposite the bus stop, spared visitors that long, exposed walk along Neo Tiew Crescent. Sungei Buloh now stretched to Kranji Way, beside Kranji Reservoir Park. There was also a mangrove gallery, a couple of terrific viewing platforms and a simple, guided path for children to follow.

Two new trails – along the coastline and the fringe of the forest – were fabulous, mostly for their superbly daft viewing towers. They were wooden, slatted, oval pods, with a winding staircase through the middle, providing shaded views of the Kranji waterfront and the Johor skyline. From a distance, they reminded me of something found at the bottom of a rabbit's hutch. That's not to downplay the value of the quirky lookout posts and their ability to manage the increased number of visitors whilst minimising the impact on the fragile mangrove eco-systems. But the pods did look like rabbit droppings.

I followed the boardwalk that jutted out across the Johor Strait, snaked through the mudflats and rose up to its highest point at the Kingfisher Pod, which was where I spotted the crocodile. The conditions were perfect. Both the tide and the sun were out. He was caked in mud and sunbathing on the bank, his claws sinking in the boggy swamp. He was my first spontaneous, unexpected crocodile encounter. In the past, Sungei Buloh staff had tipped me off if there was a "freshie"

foraging along the riverbanks, but this discovery belonged to me
– and a Malaysian chap who had sidled along the boardwalk's
railing to join me.

"It's a crocodile," I blurted out, dazzling him with my powers
of observation.

"Yah, not very big," he sniffed. "In Malaysia, got much bigger
crocodiles."

"You from Malaysia then?"

"Yah, working nearby."

"Well, the crocodile is quite big," I insisted.

"No, I've seen much bigger ones in Malaysia."

I leapt to the defence of my adopted country.

"You wouldn't want him hanging off your foot."

"Ah, it's just a baby."

"Singapore has bigger crocodiles, too, this is just one of our
smaller crocodiles."

The Malaysian wished me well and left, before I started
singing *Majulah Singapura*. Another enthusiastic wildlife spotter
soon joined me on the boardwalk. I checked his passport first.

"Hey, are you Singaporean?" I enquired.

"Yah, stay in Jurong, but I work outside," he replied.

"Ah, good," I said cheerily. "What do you think of our native
buaya? Not bad, right?"

"So small ah," he shrugged.

"Bloody hell, not you as well," I muttered.

He eyed me curiously.

"Eh?"

"I mean he's quite big right, for a Singapore crocodile."

"Ah, can be bigger."

"What for?"

"Inside got much bigger. Last time, inside Sungei Buloh, I saw
one at least 300kg."

How did he know? Did he weigh him? I was getting rather perturbed by fellow visitors ridiculing the size of my wild discovery.

In truth, the crocodile was on the petite side. From snout tip to tail, he barely stretched past 1.3m, but he was the most exclusive, and certainly the oldest, representative of Old Singapore that I'd come across and I was reluctant to leave. From the boardwalk, I followed him as he eventually roused from his slumber and meandered along the riverbank before slipping silently into the murky brown water. His protruding snout left the faintest of v-shaped ripples behind his head as he glided towards the other side of the river, towards the boardwalk, towards me. In tracking his journey across the boardwalk, I hadn't realised I had made my way down the staircase from the Kingfisher Pod and along a platform that hovered just above the water. The exposed bank was over my shoulder. All that separated me from the crocodile's intended destination was foot speed.

I didn't run. But I was guilty of a bum-cheek-squeezing power walk all the way back to the Sungei Buloh entrance.

Still, we are improving, aren't we? We're preserving and sharing space with others. Sungei Buloh Wetland Reserve continues to lead the way in educating New Singapore about what's left of Old Singapore, reminding the recalcitrant of the historical and even moral value of respecting our neighbours. Singapore is still a city with protected mangroves and wild crocodiles within its borders. That's something to celebrate and cherish, rather than shoot and destroy.

Later that evening, I proudly revealed the camera photos of my rare encounter off Singapore's northern coast to my wife. The grainy, pixelated images required some explanation as they were taken from quite a distance with an inadequate lens.

"Oh, it's a crocodile," my wife said. "I thought it was a gecko."

PRINCE WILLIAM kept me in Kranji a little longer. In late 2012, curiosity had dragged me along to Gardens by the Bay, which the Duke and Duchess of Cambridge were visiting as part of their three-day tour of Singapore. I suspected there might be a newspaper column in it so I found myself jostling for space among the multitudes beneath the harsh mid-morning sunshine. The crowd was almost exclusively white, mostly female and entirely affluent. It was as if a JCB digger had scooped up the Wimbledon tennis crowd and their strawberries and dumped them in Gardens by the Bay. They waved Union Jack flags and giggled like schoolgirls in *A Hard Day's Night* as the royal specks approached in an NParks buggy. Rather than trigger a bout of patriotic nostalgia, the royal visit had the opposite effect. I felt alien. I didn't fit in. When the royal couple eventually arrived, I just found myself admiring Prince William's fortitude as he perspired heavily in a formal suit and wondering if he'd end up with a sunburnt head. (He did.)

But the Cambridge family ended their Singapore tour with a pit stop at a historic location that I had never visited. Reading the newspaper reports the next morning, I was struck by the observations of Major (Ret) Abdul Samad from the Singapore Armed Forces Veterans' League. The 69-year-old expressed his gratitude to the royal couple for raising awareness for an overlooked landmark. And he was right.

So now I heaved my sweating body along the gentle incline of War Memorial Road and stopped before the imposing archway of the Kranji War Memorial. I was vaguely aware of the place, but had little idea of its poignant elegance and its sheer scale. I passed beneath the archway and the four school buses parked near the entrance and signed the memorial register. Visitors from Austria, England, Ireland and Australia, as well as Singapore, had already signed the book that morning. I stepped back into the wilting heat, which now seemed like a trivial concern, and made my way up the grassy, immaculately maintained slope with thousands of military graves laid out in precise rows on either side of the cemetery, almost 4,500 of them. The imagery was so overwhelming that I felt a lump tugging at the throat. The senseless loss of young lives was inescapable. I had read an information panel explaining that soldiers were buried together regardless of rank. Privates were placed beside lieutenants and so on. Only in death did these men find equality.

On the top of the Kranji hill sat the war memorial. The architectural structure had 13 columns representing the army, the wing-shaped roof acknowledged the air force and the sharp point in the middle of the roof, designed to resemble the conning tower of a submarine, was a tribute to the navy. As the memorial was opened in 1946, one could be forgiven for assuming it was devoted to British and Allied forces, but it really wasn't. Chinese, Malay and Indian names were prominent on the memorial walls that commemorated the 24,000 servicemen whose bodies were never found. The most striking observation was the number of Indian names. They were everywhere. Almost 50 per cent of those named on the memorial were Indian.

When I visited, classes from an all-girl school had been divided into small groups and sat in front of a different memorial wall as a teacher explained the significance of the names on the wall, highlighting personal stories where possible. They emphasised not only the identities of a former imperial power, but also those of an embryonic nation. So many Singaporeans were up on those walls.

It's hard not to get a little frustrated. Singapore's modern history didn't begin in 1959 or 1965. Another chapter was written, certainly, perhaps a decisive chapter, definitive even. But it wasn't the first chapter. Singapore's history was written by the victors, but we're not all on the same page any more. The rising wave of nostalgia and an increasing interest in heritage sites and historic buildings is perhaps not only a sense of yearning for a lost Singapore, but also recognition that neither 1959 nor 1965 marked Year One. The history of the People's Action Party is no less remarkable, but it isn't the only history on offer. Courage and personal sacrifice were not personal qualities monopolised by a small political elite. These strengths existed before 1959. They made 1959 possible. The common narrative will continue to focus on life after 1959, and particularly after 1965, to reiterate Singapore's sunny dawn after all that imperial darkness. But in the simplistic "before and after" potted histories that tend to dominate, there is a risk of the Kranji War Memorial being pushed into the dusty "before" section of modern history, a footnote to a wilfully forgotten past. It's already happening. Most Singaporeans I know have never visited. Far too many have never heard of the landmark (ironically, some remember that Singapore's first two presidents are buried in the adjacent State Cemetery, which is again post-1965 history). In all the campaigns and features on Singapore's 50th anniversary that I've come across, the Kranji War Memorial was never mentioned. It just doesn't fit the slender narrative.

That's such a shame because the cemetery is a fitting, dignified tribute to thousands of Singapore heroes, both local and foreign. As a final resting place, a Kranji hillside overlooking the Johor Strait takes some beating. Currently, the Commonwealth War Graves Commission maintains the splendid grounds and deserves the recognition. It seems wrong that Major (Ret) Abdul Samad was right. The Kranji War Memorial is special. But we shouldn't need Prince William to tell us that.

I was a long way away and using a phone camera at Sungei Buloh Wetland Reserve, but don't be fooled. This is a man-eating crocodile. All right, it's a crocodile.

If only Singapore's other cemeteries were treated with the same respect and dignity as Kranji War Cemetery.

Eighteen

IN 1969, Man sent a rocket to the Moon. In 1969, a man also sent a rocket to Upper Seletar Reservoir. It's time our man was recognised for his contribution to daft architecture. The late Goh Peng Koon was a draftsman working for the Public Utilities Board in the late '60s, when he clearly got caught up in the international space race. While the Americans and the Russians fought to produce the best rocket, Goh was quietly fine-tuning his own audacious design for Singapore. Like much of the architecture of the period, his rocket was offbeat, but highly original. And when he was finished, he dropped the space-age object at the foot of Seletar Reservoir.

Singaporeans had never seen anything like it.

The lookout tower still looks unusual now. When I caught a glimpse of Goh's work for the first time, I thought I was hallucinating. I was certainly dizzy. The walk had been foolishly protracted and unnecessary. Rather than wait for the No. 138 bus that services Upper Seletar Reservoir, I impetuously decided to savour the forest view as I sauntered along Mandai Road with my backpack. After 20 minutes, my sweat had turned to superglue, the backpack had melded to my skin and my chafing groin kept slapping against my upper thigh, producing that scratchy, hissing noise that frying bacon makes on a barbecue.

Singapore is too hot, really. Perhaps it's psychosomatic or I'm overanalysing or just getting older, but each island tour seems sweatier and stickier than the one before. As I trudged through Mandai Road, persistent beads of perspiration stung my eyes and cascaded down my waterslide of a chest before forming unattractive stalactites of sweat beneath my testicles. I'm not trying to be coarse but simply paint an accurate picture of my discomfort. At my wit's end, I threw down my bag, checked no one was around and liberally applied talcum powder to my affected area as I admired the view (of the reservoir, not my affected area). Even my lotions and potions had been borrowed from Old Singapore on this heritage tour. The talcum powder works a treat, but it does leave my backside looking like a powdery doughnut.

By the time I crossed the exposed dam that separates Upper Seletar Reservoir (maximising limited resources for all) from the golf course (wasting limited resources on a few towkays), I was closing in on heatstroke. I was jabbering away to the fish, dancing with the stars and chasing after rockets in the distance. I think the last one was real.

Even now, the Upper Seletar tower seemed weird and otherworldly. Opened in 1969 to celebrate both the reservoir's huge expansion and Singapore's 150th anniversary of the Raffles Landing, the six-storey design incorporated the "reach for the stars" idealism of the time and the rise of architectural brutalism. The rocket's grey, concrete exterior had a classic timber spiral staircase running through the body and was topped with a domed, flying saucer-shaped roof. When Early Man hurls a bone in the air and it turns into a spaceship in that magnificent jump-cut in *2001: A Space Odyssey*, well, the lookout tower could be that spaceship.

It could've also been open. The tower was closed for maintenance work. I wandered along the path and came across a wedding couple taking photos. Their photographer had positioned them on top of a muddy crane engine. They were going for that arty juxtaposition of funky urbanism with a classic, rural backdrop. It's a popular shot in Australia too, with bridegrooms wearing Hugo Boss suits whilst sitting on a farmer's tractor. I always found the stark contrast to be unsettling: an Australian in a Hugo Boss suit.

I watched the photographer expertly adjust the bride's dress and move the groom along the crane a little.

"Congratulations," I called out to the happy couple.

"Thank you," replied the young Chinese guy.

I nodded towards the huge, filthy crane. "I hope that's not your wedding car."

"No, this is not the wedding car," he replied. "We have a different wedding car."

I smiled at the bride and wished her the best of luck.

There was a small park between the tower and the reservoir, with just a few sheltered benches and a neat lawn where a second wedding party was finishing their photo shoot. After 45 years, Upper Seletar Reservoir Park remains an unbeatable location for a wedding album. It seems almost unfair to compare the views offered by the rocket tower with the green penis tower of Toa Payoh. One has a tranquil, undisturbed vista filled with nature reserves, forest, the Singapore Zoo and the sun's spangles dashing across the vast reservoir. And the other has a traffic jam. Of course the rocket wins. It's not the most accessible of locations, but therein lies the charm. Once the wedding parties left, I was left with my sandwiches for half an hour on a Saturday afternoon. The solitude was sublime and just about impossible anywhere else in Singapore. I was alone with my rocket, a space oddity in Upper Seletar. I stretched out to savour the silence and soothe my talcum-powdered testicles.

A LARGE Chinese construction worker in grubby jeans and muddy boots was sitting on a garden swing, rocking backwards and forwards, eating a cream bun and seriously enjoying himself. His belly peeked out from the bottom of a filthy white top and flopped over his jeans. A yellow hardhat kept him company on the swing. A Bodhi tree provided shade, its long, gnarled branches covering the swing and much of the unkempt lawn. Some litter bounced across the grass. There was garden furniture dotted around the garden, plastic tables and chairs that were once white but now as grey as the dust-caked parasols overhead. Cones were laid out haphazardly around the grass, presumably to keep vehicles away, and a couple of shaded wooden tables had been deemed a smoking corner for half a dozen construction workers who were puffing their way towards lung failure. The droning cicadas kept the squeaking garden swing company. All else was silent. The Chinese guy continued to swing in his private playground, biting chunks of cream bun and smiling like a schoolboy as he rocked back and forth.

I started to get a little excited.

Maybe I had… Maybe it was… I didn't even want to think it, in case I was wrong. I left my Chinese swinger and followed the scruffy path towards a rusting hut that was a mishmash of zinc slabs thrown on the roof and shoved against the sides to give a passable impression of four walls. Maybe the building hadn't been knocked down yet. On a large piece of zinc, the spray-painted words read: "BLK 398 CANTEEN." I quickened my stride. The building was still standing. That was something at least. I passed another hand-painted "canteen" sign, following its arrow and turning right towards the side of the hut, where a couple of motorbikes had been parked beneath a shady awning. There was a darkened opening. It was barely visible inside, but the door was obviously open. It couldn't be, could it? Every news article, every feature, every blog, every photo essay said this place would be demolished by 2015.

But it was open.

To my genuine disbelief, its plucky occupiers had defied New Singapore's band of bulldozers once more. It was still open. Shocked, I stepped into the last kampong kopitiam in the country.

Whether that moniker is factually correct is a moot point. The Block 398 Canteen at the end of Piccadilly Road represents what's left of a lost world. Its ongoing fight for survival epitomises not only the battle of its immediate community – the decimated Seletar village – but the wider war being fought between the economists and the new wave romantics. Only those with a heart of stone could not be warmed by the unique tale of Singapore's last kampong kopitiam.

In 1969, the current (and last) occupier Toh Ee Cheng joined his brother at 398 Canteen, named after its location at 398 Piccadilly Road, in the heart of the Seletar Camp. First they served the British, then dished up *hor fun* for young Singaporean soldiers from the original Seletar Camp before it shifted. Now they made tea and coffee for the labour force at the encroaching Singapore Aerospace Park and the trucks of workers reshaping the landscape around the airport.

When I last visited the Seletar Estate for *Final Notes from a Great Island*, I went for the quirky British road names like Piccadilly Circus, Oxford Street and Lambeth Walk but found a vibrant, bohemian community of (mostly wealthy) artists, architects, interior designers and so forth. The black and white bungalows made up an exclusive, gated community, but they were an alternative at least. And now, of course, most of them are gone. Wandering around roads with great names like Old Birdcage Walk and Baker Street and seeing those bungalows replaced with industrial buildings and aerospace companies was awful. All of which made the discovery of 398 Canteen so unexpected.

Even the name tickled me. Having traipsed around the gentrified districts of Tiong Bahru and Balestier, I was beginning to think every Singaporean eatery now had to be called Boulangerie de Bollocks. But No. 398 Piccadilly was home to 398 Canteen. It does what it says on the tin.

And the tin came from the 1960s, along with everything else. As I ducked my head beneath the low entrance, I walked into yesterday. The coffee shop was dark and dingy with no lights on. None of the tables and chairs matched. They were round, rectangular, red and white and had nothing in common apart from age. At the nearest table, four Chinese workers giggled at me. At another table, a trio of Indian diners gestured towards me and grinned. There were three serving counters, but only one was being used, a poignant reminder of the establishment's decline since the army camp moved away. At the back of the coffee shop, I counted six fridges, all different shapes and sizes and all wrapped in cellophane, as if waiting to be sent off to a fridge museum. The furniture, the display cabinets, the counters, the signage, the fans, fridges and clocks and even the light switches all belonged to the coffee shop's heyday. The place didn't replicate the 1960s. It was the 1960s.

At the counter, I bought a bottle of Kickapoo and a sandwich for $2 (never mind the rest of Singapore, that was cheaper than Batam). The guy introduced himself as Toh Ee Cheng. I told him how thrilled I was that his coffee shop was still around and explained the purpose of my visit.

"You an author?" he asked.

I nodded, theatrically throwing my hair back in a windswept fashion.

"Yah. We had an author here before. American guy. Very handsome."

I put my cap back on.

"So you've been here for all those years?"

"Since 1969 with my brother," he said proudly. "Apart from two years National Service, I been here my whole life."

"That's amazing. Do you think you can survive?"

"It's difficult because…"

"Kopi," his wife interrupted. She was serving another customer.

Mr Toh stole a glance at his 398 Canteen partner and then tried again.

"It's difficult because the SLA…"

"Kopi, ah."

Mr Toh turned towards his wife.

"He's an author you know."

Mr Toh pointed at the tall *ang moh* on the other side of the counter. His wife looked at me. Then she stared at her husband.

"*Kopi!*"

Mr Toh jumped and busied himself with the coffee machine. I fell in love with them both. I was a child again, on my tiptoes, leaning over the canteen counter and watching my grandparents argue over the teacups.

"That counter from the British," Mr Toh said, joining me at the table after fulfilling his wife's order. "It came from the army, you know, the Mess, the British army mess. That's the original bar, they used to sit there at one time."

"But everything's original in this place, right?"

"Everything. The roof, the walls, the counter, nothing change since 1969. In Singapore, where got? Nowhere. We are the last one."

"Can survive or not?" I asked. "I thought you were already closed down."

"We should be dead already. First it was 2012, then 2013, now we don't know. This area is controlled by the SLA (Singapore Land Authority). Last time, gave us three year renewal, then one year renewal, now just one month. They can take back any time."

"But it's been in your family since 1969."

Mr Toh sat up and pointed towards the window. "See over there, St Martin Lane, used to be whole village for the workers, everyone who worked for the British forces. My parents had a coffee shop there before they shifted here. My whole life is just two streets. Go somewhere else for what? My children grown up already, can make enough here to survive, no stress, peaceful. If they close, we retire."

I finished my drink and got up to leave. Mr Toh shook my hand.

"Good luck," I said, rather feebly.

"Don't need luck, I need the SLA," he grinned.

"Kopi!" his wife bellowed.

As I bounded along Piccadilly, trying to filter out the din of distant diggers, I basked in the glory of my discovery. I had found rare treasure, a genuine golden oldie, still in working order, but only just. Ignoring those bloody drillers at the nearby aerospace park, I was determined to remain upbeat. I realised I was wrong. Mr Toh doesn't need luck. He needs you. He needs visitors. Let's not wait for the patronising black and white photo exhibition when 398 Canteen is gone. Let's have a stab at saving the old place while the bugger's still standing. Urban planners need a reason for the coffee shop to stay open beyond some wishy-washy mumbling about heritage and a sustained connection to a community's past. They need figures. The statisticians struggle with figures they cannot control. At least make it hard for them. Vote with your feet. Pop down to Piccadilly and buy a bun from Singapore's last *kampong* kopitiam.

But do hurry.

In 1969, the Americans put a rocket on the Moon in the Space Race. In 1969, Singapore put a rocket at Upper Seletar Reservoir. It's not the winning. It's the taking part that counts.

Singapore's last kampong kopitiam in Piccadilly Road may not be around for much longer. But if it is, pop in for a bun and a Kickapoo. Go today.

Nineteen

MY FAMILY and Singapore's famous Cashin family have something in common. Go back far enough along the family tree and you'll eventually reach a drug dealer. For obvious reasons, I can say no more. (I'm not worried about offending the Cashin family. I'm terrified of my mother.) But the famous Irish family first settled in Singapore in the 1840s, made a fortune from investing in opium farms in the 1880s, which were then legal, before moving into property. The Cashins owned more than 400 shophouses at one point and several luxurious seafront properties including, of course, The Pier, tucked away in the Lim Chu Kang swamp. For my book, *Return to a Sexy Island*, I visited the Cashin's dilapidated coastal retreat and found myself getting lost in the swamp and using a wicker basket-shaped tree stump to make a biodegradable deposit. So the Cashins and I share a bit of history.

The Cashins also built Matilda House in Punggol. When researching my previous book, I read about the historical bungalow, which was reportedly built in 1902 by Alexander Cashin. I was struck by a touching article, where a reporter from *The New Paper* took Alexander's son, Howard Cashin, back to his childhood home in 2002. By then an old man himself, Howard was visibly distressed. Matilda House was falling apart. With Punggol earmarked for massive residential development, Matilda House had been returned to the Urban Redevelopment Authority. One of Singapore's oldest houses was granted conservation status in 2000 and then left to rot. While the new towns of Punggol and the neighbouring Sengkang took root and reached for the sky in less than a decade, Matilda House was largely forgotten. A Google image search invariably throws up a sad photograph from the previous decade. Matilda House stands alone on state land in an unkempt Punggol field, with Soo Teck LRT station looming large in the background. It's one of my favourite photos. The symbolism is striking. The LRT has arrived. The apartment blocks are coming. The future is now. Matilda House is a dying species, out of touch with the rapidly evolving environment. It's Singapore's ongoing war of the worlds in one photo. Besides, my previous book was a tour of sexy, sparkly New Singapore. There was no place for a rusty, collapsing slum.

But Matilda House is just about all Punggol has left of Old Singapore. So I made my way from Soo Teck LRT station to the town's last bungalow fearing the worst. I had read that a property developer had bought the site and, to the Government's credit, been ordered to restore and maintain Matilda House as one of the sale conditions. But how could a colonnade of condos not swallow up the antiquated property?

I passed through the recently opened, and extremely well appointed, HDB estate, skipped around the playground and there it was, right in front of me. Only a green fence separated us.

Matilda House looked spectacular.

I was aware that the property would host the condo development's clubhouse, but the bungalow was clearly being positioned as the aesthetic centerpiece rather than an unwanted afterthought. The red roof had been retiled and stretched across the staircases on either side of the home. The building had obviously been impeccably restored and repainted and the verandah offered an imposing entrance. Workers planted trees and bushes and busied themselves with the garden (which had obviously shrunk considerably from the home's heyday, when the sprawling lawns led to a beach just 200m away). The adjacent condos didn't overwhelm Matilda House, but in fact had the opposite effect. The old house stood out more in a maddening crowd.

A youngish Chinese couple stood beside me and peered through the fence.

"Have you bought a place here?" I asked cheerily.

They noticed my notepad.

"Er, maybe, looking into it," the guy stammered. "We're not sure yet."

"You know this is a historic site, right?"

"Is it?"

"That's Matilda House."

The couple blankly stared at me. The guy eyed me curiously.

"I thought it was the clubhouse."

"No, no, it is the clubhouse, but it's Matilda House, the last bungalow in Punggol. If you buy here, you're buying a piece of history."

"Are you a property agent?"

It was a fair question. My enthusiasm was at the point of combustion. But I was pleased that Matilda House had been so sensitively restored. Of course, as I watched the small army of underpaid and unappreciated foreign workers place tiles around the barbecue pits, I was aware of who would be bringing the satay sticks in the future. Matilda House now belonged, pretty much exclusively, to the wealthier classes (as it always had). But Singapore is so short of plausible alternatives. If the only other choices are demolish the building or wait a decade or two and then demolish the building, then integrating historic properties with modern housing projects is a workable compromise (a similar agreement is in place for Marine Parade's Sea Breeze Lodge, opposite Parkway Parade). At the time of writing, Matilda House hosts a lounge and a gymnasium. The Cashins' other bungalow, The Pier at Lim Chu Kang, hosts pigeons. It's Hobson's choice.

As I followed the perimeter fencing to admire the main balcony on the other side of Matilida House, I met a middle-aged guy. He was more forthcoming.

"I bought an apartment here," he said, whilst taking photographs with his phone. "Got a good price last time, before they increase the stamp duty. You buy one?"

"No, no, I just like the clubhouse."

"I heard it's quite old right?"

It was an open invitation. I regaled the poor man with a detailed potted history of the Cashin family, Matilda House, the Pier, the 400 shophouses and the once legal opium farms.

"Wah, interesting ah," he admitted. "So that clubhouse is the last bungalow left in Punggol?

"Yep, the very last one."

He nodded to himself as he absorbed the information. Then his eyes widened.

"Will that increase the value of my unit?"

I AM AN ENTHUSIASTIC CYCLIST. Some of my best friends are cyclists. And yet, a number of cyclists are committed to giving the rest of us a bad name. They are not smart people. Their brains must rattle like a pea in a whistle. After many years of jumping out of the way of the dopey buggers, I have developed a conspiracy theory about certain cyclists in Singapore. One day, the Government decided to introduce the Certificate of Entitlement for car owners to keep only the educated, wealthy elite on the road. Everyone else took public transport. But there were still exceptions. There was that small minority of folks who staggered onto the pavements to excitedly point at the moon each evening. They were not trusted with COE documents or a bus pass. Oh no. They were each handed a bicycle with a bell.

These people should not be trusted with bicycles and bells. These people should not be trusted with soft toilet paper.

Singapore has erred in its transport strategy. For a while, the island just about got away with it. Most people were crammed onto cars, trains and buses and the pedal pushers were largely out of sight, out of mind. But then, the population exploded, infrastructure creaked and alternative modes of transport were explored and encouraged. Park connectors were expanded and linked, with an islandwide cycling-path network to be completed by 2030.

And then, someone did the unthinkable. He covered his wobbly body in Lycra and incorrectly assumed he looked cool. He saw Lycra Man. Everyone else saw a flaccid penis struggling to escape a technicolour condom. But he saw Lycra Man. He quickly inspired others to follow him. Soon, there were Lycra men and women everywhere, zooming past the pedalling platoons of factory workers and terrorising commuters foolishly waiting at bus stops.

And they are always ringing that fucking bell.

Do not give these people a bell. A bell issues a warning, an order. A bell is both an instrument of terror and an aural display of power. A ring on that bell denotes a clear distinction in passing relationships. The bell listener is a minion. The bell ringer is a moron.

And yet, the Government wants more bell ringers. Current estimates suggest that cycling makes up only 2 per cent of transport modes in Singapore (that's already a lot of bell ringers), but there is a concerted effort to increase that figure, to send more innocent pedestrains spinning like a top at bus stops as the uneasy riders go thundering past on the pavements. That's the most entertaining irony regarding the born-again, hardcore bikers. They dress as steroid-addicted, muscular machines preparing for the mountain climbs of the Tour de France. But they cycle with all the timidity of a toddler still using stabilisers, pedalling on the pavement because Mummy insists that only grown-ups are allowed on the road. I am aware of the absence of cycling lanes on Singapore's roads and the unwritten rules of the Highway Code (never use the mirror, never signal, always manoeuvre, intimidate anything smaller, slower or cheaper and hit the horn for all of the above). But pulling on the full Lycra bodysuit to ride through a bus stop is rather like throwing on a fireman's uniform to blow out the candles on a birthday cake.

As I fought my way through the otherwise lovely Punggol Promenade, I dodged cyclists, scooters, tandems, twosomes, threesomes and the various other metallic contraptions that rental outlets have come up with to knock pedestrians into the Serangoon Harbour. I am now firmly of the view that prospective bike renters should take a simple intelligence test before being unleashed on Singapore's unsuspecting parks and gardens. Nothing too strenuous, they haven't got to know the first five American presidents, just their left from their right.

Clearly, NParks has gone to considerable expense to mark out cycling paths and connectors across the country, with a pair of clown-sized feet and a stick man on a bicycle stencilled onto the smooth tarmac at regular intervals to demarcate the different lanes for walkers and riders. They demarcate nothing. I became an unwitting participant in my own video game, jumping from side to side like Super Mario on speed. It was as if the bicycle renters had gathered for a private meeting beforehand and said:

"You see how there's a pair of elephantine feet and an anorexic rider painted on the floor to tell us which lane to use? Fuck it. Let's do the opposite. That'll freak out the *ang moh*."

One particular guy, who navigated his rented bike in the way you and I might navigate a Boeing 747, careened towards me on the footpath. He didn't correct his steering. He rang his bell instead.

"That's it, ring that bell, Quasimodo," I shouted towards him. "You've almost got the hang of it. Have you been taking lessons?"

We dodged a collision only because I jumped out of my lane and into the path for cyclists, where I narrowly avoided stepping on a kid powering past on a tricycle. As he whizzed past, I suggested where he might stick his bloody bell (Quasimodo, not the kid on the tricycle).

It's important not to tarnish all cyclists with Quasimodo's bell of course. Punggol Point used to be a remote, smelly and rather unpleasant place that was seldom visited by anyone other than fishermen and illegal immigrants from Indonesia. But I visited on a beautifully balmy Saturday evening and the entire promenade from Punggol Beach to Coney Island was abuzz with physical activity. Joggers, cyclists and retirees taking a stroll had breathed life into the old place.

And the traffic will eventually be steered onto Coney Island, the reason for my visit. By the end of 2015, the green gem will be open to the public. In the past, fishermen and picnickers often visited the island, covering the short 100m stretch of water by boat from neighbouring Punggol or Changi Point. Kelongs once dotted the horizon lines and water-skiers sped past, but the island remained undeveloped and uninhabited beyond migratory birds treating the blissful retreat as a transit lounge. But Pulau Serangoon, to use its older name, will see about half the island reserved for a rustic, natural haven, with a bird-watching sanctuary, ecologically sensitive walkways and discreet, unimposing solar-powered lights, as part of an Urban Redevelopment Authority Master Plan. So far, so sensible.

And the other part of the island is zoned for – come on, say it with me – residential use. On the plus side, the land isn't immediately required for development so will be left alone as an interim park for now. But the island barely covers 45 hectares. Even my favourite Singaporean eccentrics, the Aw brothers of Haw Par Villa fame, realised the place was not quite large enough and sold the island. Other entrepreneurs came on board in the 1950s and considered the theme park option (hence the Coney Island moniker), but they decided it was better left alone. It's too big to ignore and neglect, but far too small to overly develop. Even real estate researchers have opposed the idea of clearing all that lush vegetation to plonk high-end residential units on the island's fringes to give owners dusky views of the sand barges and silos and all the industrial crap that piles up on the Punggol shoreline when the tide goes out. It's surely counterproductive. An open, accessible, protected Coney Island is an attractive selling point for homeowners in Punggol and Sengkang. It doesn't quite work the other way round.

But the rustic nature park with boardwalks and play areas made from recycled casuarina trees found on the island sounds promising; a rational compromise between Old and New Singapore. There will also be bike racks. So there will be bikes. We might have to grab them by the bells. Or something like that.

Rather than dwarf Punggol's last bungalow, the condos around Matilda House amplify its elegance. That should do wonders for property prices, too.

Coney Island should be opened up to the public, but beware the bikes.

Twenty

THE KID in all of us loves an underground tunnel. It's the heady mix of suspense and fear that comes with stepping into the darkness and wondering what's in there with us. Enid Blyton's Famous Five were always finding underground tunnels. They couldn't park their bikes without falling into a tunnel. At primary school, my class was led into a proper Enid Blyton-type tunnel beneath a gothic Victorian manor house in the leafy Suffolk countryside. It was one of the greatest trips of my school life. Ringsfield Hall was (and remains, I was delighted to discover online) an outward bounds eco-centre for schools in the south of England. Set in 25 acres of woodland, the house was a rural wonderland for dumbstruck kids from London's housing estates.

It was where I developed a taste for the outdoors.

It was also where Christopher Wells smacked his head open.

After a week of camping, exploring, writing and drawing, school groups were rewarded with a trip to the underground tunnel. It ran beneath the manor house and was at least a hundred years old when I visited. Ringsfield Hall's benevolent proprietor opened a wooden hatch and directed us down a staircase one at a time, advising us to stay low to avoid the timber beams supporting the property's foundations. With boyish enthusiasm,

I dashed inside and Chris followed. The tunnel was small and claustrophobic and the caliginous conditions genuinely unsettling – all of which we hid behind prepubescent bravado, of course.

"Chris, Chris," I whispered. "Isn't this place brilliant?"

"Yeah, brilliant," a voice echoed along the narrow walkway. "Do you reckon there are bats above us…"

Whack.

"Argh… Neil… Neil," the same voice cried. "I've hit me fucking head."

I stopped.

"How did you do that?"

"The bats."

I ducked in the darkness.

"You were hit by a bat?"

"No, I tried to stand up to see if there were any bats and smacked my head on the beam."

"Does it hurt?"

"It's fucking killing me."

The trouble was we'd only just started and still had to navigate our way through the rest of the tunnel. With a dozen kids behind us in a confined space, retreating wasn't an option. We had to plough on through the pitch-black labyrinth. This terrifying, ghoulish groaning followed me at every turn.

"Ooh… Ooh… Argh… Ooh…"

"Will you stop doing that? You're scaring the shit out of me."

"Neil, Neil, I think I'm dying, Neil."

"And I think I've got a ghost chasing me."

"There's blood pouring down my face, Neil… It's going in my eyes… Neil, Neil… I can't see a thing, Neil."

"No one can see, Chris. We're in an underground tunnel."

It wasn't very Enid Blyton. When we finally emerged into the daylight of the old scullery, Chris did indeed have the most startling appearance. Attempting to stem the bloody geyser gushing from his forehead, he had wiped dusty, soot-covered hands all over his face. Some of the other children ran away. A couple of the girls screamed. Even the Ringsfield Hall proprietor took a step back.

Finally, Chris grabbed a tissue, wiped the blood from his face and said: "That was great, sir, can me and Neil have another go?"

I tell this story to hopefully convey my lifelong love for underground tunnels, historic bunkers and silly subterranean adventures and, most of all, to underline what a spectacularly underwhelming experience the Johore Battery was.

I had such high hopes for the place. Having visited Fort Siloso and the old Ford Factory, my admiration for the work of the relevant statutory boards had increased considerably. And Johore Battery's rediscovery was a tale of genuine intrigue. In 1991, the Prisons Department Singapore discovered tunnels in the Abingdon Centre at Changi that led to a concrete bunker three storeys deep. Further digging revealed that it was an ammunition bunker for a 15-inch "monster" gun. There were more tunnels, too, revealing an elaborate ammunition store. It was front-page news at the time. When the Johore Battery was installed in the 1930s, its three 15-inch guns were among the island's largest coastal guns. On 12th February 1942, the British destroyed the guns shortly before surrendering. And the site was pretty much forgotten about until 1991. It was one hell of a find. So I anticipated an underground, concrete military complex with a maze of tunnels and ammunition racks; the perfect picnic spot for the Famous Five.

I found a seafood restaurant with a fake gun by a car park.

I thought I had arrived at the wrong place. Having cycled for nearly two hours, via East Coast Park, the Changi Coast Road, Changi Beach Park, Loyang Avenue, Loyang Way and

Upper Changi Road North – all without the aid of a bell – I was unimpressed when I pulled over at the bend where the roads of Abingdon and Cosford met. The map indicated Johore Battery's location. I saw an upmarket seafood restaurant advertising its daily specials. The site was otherwise forlorn, rather pitiful and deserted. As it was a Monday, even the restaurant was closed. A small, whitewashed hut, which was open, had some interesting information on its peeling walls. But the panels had faded. So had the Johore Battery. Behind the hut, the monster 15-inch gun – painted green and black – was an imperious sight. It was also a replica. But the gun was at least on its actual site and still had a function. The restaurant's dustbins had been stacked against its rear.

Some concrete paths marked out the tunnels beneath, but they were cracked, crumbling and covered by grass. There was no access; no signboards, plaques or heritage signs that I could see. One tiny section was covered with Perspex instead of concrete, inviting visitors to press a button to illuminate the tunnel beneath. The light didn't work. There really was nothing to see here.

Considering the nation's 50th anniversary celebrations were leaving no historic stone unturned, the neglect of such a significant World War II site was surprising. Perhaps it's another relic that falls outside of the 1965-2015 parameters. With a bit of luck, the seafood restaurant might bring curious visitors back to the Johore Battery.

Nothing else will.

MY WIFE'S FRIEND was adamant. I had to stay away. Even a daytime visit was a risky business.

"Don't go Old Changi Hospital," she said. "It's got ghosts."

I foolishly laughed. I thought she was joking. She wasn't.

"Hey, I'm serious," she insisted, her eyes boring through me.

"I heard so many ghosts story before. There are a lot around Changi from last time, got many ghosts around the army camps during World War II."

"Singapore had a ghost army?"

My puerile interjections were not appreciated. She's one of my wife's oldest friends, an extremely kind woman. But she did also tell us not to spend a few days at the First World Hotel, a hilltop resort in Malaysia's Genting Highlands, because ghosts lived in the clouds.

"You don't seriously believe there are ghosts flying around the hotel windows," I asked incredulously. "It's not *Ghostbusters*."

"Many people have said they have seen really strange things in Genting Highlands, especially late at night."

"So have I. They're called drunk gamblers."

We spent a few days in the Genting Highlands and the only alien object I encountered was a terrifying wig atop a Chinese uncle's head. We came down in a lift together. He turned towards me to say good morning, but his wig didn't.

We had been lucky, apparently. I should not tempt fate a second time.

"You never saw any ghosts at Genting First World," our friend reasoned. "So you will probably see them if you go to Changi."

I laughed off her juvenile concerns, cycled through old Changi, powered along Netheravon Road, dropped the bike on the path, peered up at the crumbling hospital and hummed the theme from *Ghostbusters*. I could see why the building was a popular haunt for kids with cameras looking for paranormal activity.

But first I needed to pee. From the Johore Battery to the Old Changi Hospital, I had searched in vain for a toilet. Getting off the bike seat released a convenient bladder blockage. I had to go immediately. Standing at the top of the leafy Barrack Hill,

I was reasonably secluded and a socially acceptable distance away from the odd car passing below on Netheravon Road. I skipped across the overgrown grass, ignoring the rustling of fleeing reptiles as I ran, and made use of the natural cover. I peed against an enormous tree trunk, poking my head around each side occasionally, checking for passers-by or security guards. I felt a tickle around the ankle. I ignored it. I was busy. Then I felt a gentle itch on my other ankle and my shin. I focused on the job in hand. But the tickling persisted so I peered down at my legs. They were turning red. An army of red ants had launched an invasion, eager to set up base camp around my kneecaps. I had never seen so many so quickly.

"Oh my… Shit, shit, shit."

Like a cat on a hot tin roof, I started jumping up and down. But I was still peeing. I looked like a fireman who'd lost control of his water hose. Considering the clear skies, the confused ants must have wondered where the sudden shower was coming from. I pulled up my shorts, dashed through the grass and back to the footpath, stamping my feet and pulling red ants from my socks. They were everywhere (I was still finding them in my rucksack when I returned home hours later).

But the unwelcoming ant attack felt entirely appropriate. If a movie studio instructed a set designer to build a haunted house on a hill, he would doubtlessly come up with something not too dissimilar to Old Changi Hospital. Its decaying appearance and overgrown setting befitted its grim history. Built in 1935 to serve Changi's military base, the hospital was swiftly turned into a prison camp where the Japanese Secret Police (the Kempeitai) reportedly kept a torture chamber. The building reverted to a hospital after the war until it closed in 1997 and had remained empty ever since. Picture a rotting, empty shell that once housed death and misery. That's Old Changi Hospital.

My wife's friend was right. Even in the daytime, I was jittery and very much aware of my loneliness. I made my way up the hill, very slowly, via a stone staircase that was barely visible under the weeds. I bobbed and weaved to sidestep, duck beneath or climb over tree branches and roots. Three birds of prey, brahminy kites I think, circled overhead, adding to the eeriness. At the top of the staircase, I faced a fence. A roundish hole had obviously been crudely cut beneath the barbed wire. A large slab of rock had been placed on the other side of the fence, a bizarre welcome mat. I hesitated before slipping through the hole.

Startled pigeons immediately flew from their nest in the roof of the sheltered entrance. Peeled layers of whitewash hung down from the roof's timber planks. Their blackened sides gave the appearance of hanging bats. Weeds poured through ventilation shafts and cracked window panes in every building. There were three blocks and I considered exploring the main, three-storey building. I peered through the doorway. The corridor was long and dark. Mould was making its way down the walls. I took a single step inside and a disturbed bird flapped its wings and flew across the room. I ran back into the courtyard. The Cowardly Lion has got nothing on me.

The place still had plenty of visitors though. Old Changi Hospital was a sanctuary for butterflies, birds of prey and the parakeets that are often spotted in Changi Village. Camera crews periodically turn up to film horror movies and TV ghost stories and paranormal investigators often pop up to put the abandoned hospital in their top-10 list of Singapore's most haunted places. It was undeniably spooky.

It was also being wasted. Earlier, I had passed the old commando barracks in Netheravon Road, equally old and equally "haunted" according to those so inclined, and yet the once derelict building had been tastefully transformed into a hilltop hotel overlooking Serangoon Harbour. The Old Changi Hospital boasts a similar location and merits a similar makeover. The 80-year-old buildings obviously need more than a lick of paint and a couple of trips to IKEA. But a tasteful development along the lines of the Kam Leng Hotel in Jalan Besar would breathe life into the historic site.

Just get rid of the bloody ants first.

Even in the daytime, Old Changi Hospital looks like a horror movie set. I climbed through those trees in the middle. I peed against that tree on the right.

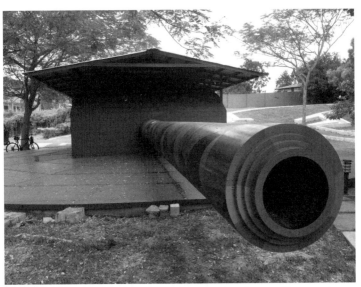

My, that's a big one. Johore Battery keeps a replica "monster" gun at the original emplacement site. Note my bike at the side. It doesn't have a bell.

Twenty One

BEING an immigrant myself, I thought it only right and proper to attend Singapore's anti-immigration rally at Hong Lim Park in 2013. I couldn't help myself. Around that time, I had interviewed one of the rally's organisers for a TV show and we got ourselves into a bit of a surreal, Monty Python-like argument. He stressed that Singapore should be primarily for Singaporeans. Naturally, I agreed. In any country, a society should primarily serve its citizens. So our discussion moved towards which foreigners should stay or go. What about me? I asked provocatively. No, I was all right, he said. What about western expats like the chap I had previously interviewed for TV, whose ad agency created 300 jobs for Singaporeans? No, he was OK. What about the domestic helpers from the Philippines, Indonesia and Myanmar? No, they could stay. What about the East Asians playing a role in our banking and electronics industries? What about our friends from South Asia working in the construction industries or providing cleaning and gardening services? What about our Causeway neighbours driving our buses for long hours for comparatively low wages? No, they were all allowed to stay. We had dipped into that classic scene from *Life of Brian*. So apart from the *ang mohs*, the Japanese, the Chinese, the South Koreans, the Filipinos, the

Indonesians, the Myanmarese, half a dozen nations across South Asia and the Malaysians next door, what have the foreigners ever done for us?

Of course, I was being a tad facetious. I empathised with the broader point on immigration and was no less shocked by the initial sardine-can figure of 6.9 million. Even as a population estimate, the number seemed too large for an island so small, with or without the necessary infrastructure.

So I attended the anti-immigration rally.

I stood amongst the "foreigners go home", "PAP go home" and "Lassie go home" banners. As I was literally head and shoulders above most of the boisterous crowd, my distant, blurry image inadvertently appeared in several newspapers the following day, a lone white face surrounded by placards essentially telling me to go "home".

A couple of tattooed, bicep-bulging chaps in tight singlets stood in front of me, waving "Singapore for Singaporeans" banners in my face. I wasn't entirely sure what they were expecting, so I complimented the artwork and suggested they paint bigger letters next time to really amplify the xenophobic message. But the surreal highlight of the anti-foreigner protest came when a young activist with a particularly belligerent slogan scrawled on a poster shouldered his way through the crowd to get to me. As he put down the poster, I braced myself for the inevitable confrontation.

"Eh, *Dumpwee*," he shouted. "I like your columns, man. Can take photo or not?"

But some citizens do feel increasingly alienated and ignored in their own country. Singapore is veering into uncharted political territory and the uncertainty is a legitimate cause for concern. The Government can no longer be sure of its large majorities from an unpredictable, strident electorate. Singaporeans feel constricted, foreigners feel unwanted and the relationship between the two remains wary and uneasy.

So the only sensible thing to do really is open a string of expat-targeted businesses around Joo Chiat.

We had our Monty Python debate about foreigners at Speakers Corner. Had the conversation taken place anywhere in the Joo Chiat area, I would not have had a post-colonial leg to stand on. Parts of the historic town feel like a Western monoculture has spread its legs and taken a dump over the Peranakan shophouses.

As I wandered through the predominately expatriate crowd, I came across long stretches filled with American bars, European bakeries and large German sausages. That's not prison talk. I wasn't chased by a flasher from Frankfurt. I was battered by the bratwurst. Multicultural variety is one thing, but this felt like an invasion. One outlet focused almost entirely on expatriate clientele, offering a special service for expats. As I stood outside the closed business on a dusky Sunday evening, the questions left me dizzy. Did they employ only expats? If so, how is that any different to "Singapore for Singaporeans"? And how did one qualify for an expat service? At the very least, I expected potential customers to offer a quick burst of *God Save the Queen,* down a yard of ale and complain about the price of imported fish fingers.

And there's the flipside to consider. Are Singaporeans denied entry to such establishments in their own street? Such services do not imply inclusivity. Perhaps the restrictive rules of entry are waived if one demonstrates a certain proclivity for expatriate tastes and habits – adopting a fake *ang moh* accent, perhaps, or eschewing local food in favour of Western brunches. (Funnily enough, some of these folks do live in the Joo Chiat area, so the market research of these businesses can't be faulted.)

But that's Joo Chiat. It's hard to know who fits and where in the historic district. It's a trendy enclave with a confused identity. Joo Chiat proudly became Singapore's first heritage town in 2011. Renovated shophouses, regular exhibitions and a popular heritage trail showcase the town's Peranakan and Eurasian history. The area has mostly thrived since Chew Joo Chiat bought the land to establish nutmeg and pepper plantations. When the affluent Straits Chinese flocked to the desirable seaside location in the 1920s, their eclectic architecture sprung up across Joo Chiat, to be one day occupied by gastro bars and KTV lounges. That's the confused identity. The area straddles both chic and sleazy.

Joo Chiat has an almost neat geographical and cultural divide either side of Dunman Road. From East Coast Road, the street is dotted with Western bars, restaurants, hair and nail salons and the occasional *patisserie de pretentious*. But as I headed north towards Geylang Road, the tired, haggard faces of haunted prostitutes glared up at me from rundown coffee shop tables. Tubby rent boys in ill-fitting jeans passed me in the street. A Malay beggar asked tourists for money outside a mosque. The wine bars and upmarket burger joints had vanished. So had the white faces. By the time I reached Geylang Road, I saw only Malay teenagers with outstanding blonde Mohawks flirting with tattooed girls outside the Joo Chiat Complex. Filipinos chatted with construction workers. A Chinese auntie collected cardboard. The street was filled with litter. Singaporeans were certainly welcome here. It was hard to believe I was still in a road of cider bars and pet groomers. For Joo Chiat, it's very much the best of times and the worst of times, depending on what side of the road you happen to call your own. It's Singapore in a single street. New Singapore thrives. Old Singapore struggles in the shadow of its shiny successor. Joo Chiat is by no means the granddaddy of gentrification. It is a curious muddle in search of a middle ground.

OR MAYBE IT'S NOT. Perhaps Joo Chiat's future is assured. I caught a glimpse of it when I took a bus along East Coast Road and visited a cultural corpse. In 2013, it was announced that four HDB blocks in the Joo Chiat constituency would be demolished under the en-bloc scheme. Ironically, they were more than 50 years old (one of the few half-centuries unlikely to be acknowledged). Apart from its age, the small Siglap Estate boasted another notable feature. Its apartments were the last HDB blocks standing in Joo Chiat. When they go, Joo Chiat becomes the first all-private-property constituency in Singapore. For a country built on a once enviable public housing policy, it feels like a pyrrhic victory for the island's economic progress.

On closer inspection, the Siglap Estate really did stand out from the crowd. The blocks were only five storeys high and perhaps the only apartments along the East Coast Road without balconies, barbecues and swimming pools. I climbed the staircase of Block 2 (there were no lifts) and stepped over a snoozing auntie in the stairwell. Like Dracula in a coffin, she sat bolt upright. She offered me some food.

"No thanks, Auntie," I said. "You stay here?"

I gestured towards the stairwell, idiotically suggesting she was sleeping rough on the concrete.

"No, stay Marine Drive," she replied. "Here I clean."

She pointed a finger at me.

"You come here for what?"

"Just to look around."

She stared at me.

"You *ang moh*."

"Yes."

"So? Come here why?"

"Er, I like history and these blocks are very old."

She shrugged.

"Finish. No more."

I wasn't sure if she was referring to the estate or our conversation. I suspected the latter as she rolled over on the concrete and closed her eyes. I continued climbing and, on one of the upper floors, came across an apartment's dusty contents thrown out onto the corridor. There was an analog TV, a rusty bike, a fridge freezer, two chests of drawers, a bed frame and a chipped, molding wardrobe. A faded Chinese calendar from 1993 was stuck to the wardrobe door. Someone's life had been left to rot in a condemned corridor. Many of the units were already boarded up. The mostly elderly residents, for so long asset-rich but cash-poor in their highly prized East Coast location, were in the process of being relocated to Chai Chee. The ties that bound them to their community for more than five decades were being severed.

But few were wallowing in piteous sentimentality. There was no point. Blubbing won't spare them. In the car park in front of Block 4, there was the unlikely sight of half a dozen gleaming black Mercedes. Their chauffeurs, dressed in white shirts and black trousers, sat around a plastic table. The car park was otherwise deserted.

"From here, it's only one traffic light to Changi Airport," a burly guy with a brutally shaved head told me. "We got cheap *makan*, no one disturb and we don't *kena* parking fine."

I watched the limo drivers come and go. The Siglap Estate's neglected car park was a clandestine meeting place for chauffeurs, a casual hangout to talk cock and avoid parking tickets. It was a fascinating community within a community.

"How do you know about this place?" I asked.

"I lived here for 20 years last time," the shaved guy replied gruffly.

"Are you sad it's coming down?" I wondered. "It's the last HDB in Joo Chiat."

Honestly, he struggled to give a shit.

"In Singapore, it's like that. We come in with nothing. We leave with nothing. And in the middle, we got politicians and policemen talking shit."

He sat back and took a long drag on his cigarette. I allowed the profundity to sink in. I was vaguely impressed with the middle-aged man until he expressed his love of "gangsterism" and revealed that the happiest years of his life were spent in Changi Prison. I bid him farewell. I was slightly scared.

I wandered around the four blocks for a bit. They were separated by the Siglap Canal and were at odds with the Javanese massages and pet grooming services on the other side of East Coast Road. Beneath blocks one and two, there were much older family businesses touting quaint, personalised services such as picture framing, photo developing and suit tailoring. The beauty salon shop sign even celebrated its air conditioning. The owners were skilled artisans armed with less relevant skills in New Singapore's off-the-peg culture. They were an endangered species fully aware of their demise. They even had a fixed date.

"I got four months," the kindly Chinese uncle told me.

He ran the photo studio with a sublime retro sign over his shop. I had gone in to buy something, anything, because I felt sorry for him. He didn't want my sympathy. He wanted my custom. He wanted his shop back. The wall behind his counter was filled with family photos.

"I've been here 45 years," he said proudly, pointing out the photos. "My son was born when I had this business and my grandson. Last time, I developed everybody's photos, take wedding photos, do studio shoots, now I sell phone cards. Most people move out already."

"Can you set up somewhere else?"

"They give me $60,000. I'll retire already, cannot afford anywhere else. My whole life was here, so I finish here."

I paid for a few birthday cards (something that is difficult to find in the gleaming, all-under-one-roof shopping malls) and wished him well in retirement. Outside his shop, I took some photos of Joo Chiat's last HDB blocks for posterity. These blocks were one of the first projects completed by HDB in 1962. They were built quickly to replace the kampongs destroyed in a fire caused by firecrackers during Chinese New Year celebrations at the old Siglap Market (one of the island's most famous in its prime. In its place stands the curvy, retro Siglap Centre, which is struggling to stay afloat). Until the condos arrived, the Siglap Estate's four blocks were prominent landmarks and close to the sea.

By the time you read this, however, they will probably be gone.

Joo Chiat will no longer have any HDB flats within its borders. The constituency will be an entirely private estate, the first in Singapore.

Still, Joo Chiat Road does have more expat eateries specialising in large German sausages. So it's not all bad news.

If you find a local eatery on this side of Joo Chiat, you might be eligible for a National Day Award. But it is the place to go if you fancy a German sausage.

By the time you read this, the Siglap Estate will probably be gone. Joo Chiat will be an entirely private estate. This is economic progress, apparently.

Twenty Two

WHEN MEETING SINGAPOREANS for the first time, I forget my skin colour. It's not something I pay much attention to. Still, when I see a Singaporean, they often see a tourist. The assumption is understandable, if wearying after a while. Tailors and money-changers are serial offenders of course. There is an elderly money changer, in the East Coast area, who sits on a stool outside his small, subdivided unit and will always, without fail, greet my passing with a cheery: "Change money? I give you good price. Come."

I pass this kindly man every day. He must be blessed with the memory of a goldfish. Or maybe I present myself as a dubious currency trader always on the lookout for cheap ringgit.

There is fun to be had in playing the dumb, wide-eyed tourist. My skin colour has led to interrogations about my employment status, my salary, the price of my apartment and my alleged sexual inadequacies (true story. A taxi driver was once surprised to learn that I only had one child because *ang mohs*, unlike the Chinese, were similar to the Malays in their preference for larger families. So, obviously, my penis wasn't working properly. That was the only available explanation. After scything my way through his foggy stereotypes, I cleared my head and wondered aloud if I might be gay. He almost crashed his taxi).

So as we stood together beside the site of the old Kallang Airport, I knew that the guy meant well. But I couldn't help myself. We had crossed paths along the sheltered walkway that connects Kallang MRT station and the Geylang bus terminal to the Singapore Sports Hub. (When I was writing *Return to a Sexy Island*, the Sports Hub was a building site filled with sand. As I write this book, the Sports Hub is a modern, functioning sports stadium with a pitch filled with sand.)

I pointed towards the exquisite Terminal Building of the old Kallang Airport. "Excuse me, that's the airport, right?" I asked eagerly.

He was puzzled.

"No, that's the old airport," he pointed out. "Our airport is now at Changi."

Slowly, I peered across at the deserted terminal building, its empty east and west blocks, the vacated hangar and the vast expanse of nothing.

"No, no, I meant it's still an airport building. It's not being used for anything else, which is good."

"It's not an airport," he emphasised, really, really seriously now. "Our airport is at Changi."

"Oh, so it's not an airport then."

I was enjoying myself now.

"No, this airport finished."

"Ah, I wasn't sure. So I cannot fly from here anymore."

He shook his head decisively.

"Cannot. It's closed a long time already."

"What about regional flights, to Phuket or Bintan?"

"No, cannot. You must go Changi Airport."

I feel obligated to point out, particularly for the benefit of non-Singaporean readers, that the Old Kallang Airport closed in 1955. I wouldn't want you turning up with suitcases intent on a shopping trip to Bangkok. The check-in times are appalling.

But she was still a graceful beauty to behold. She had those shapely, glassy curves that went out of fashion not long after prohibition. Unfortunately, the hulking, muscular Singapore Sports Hub overshadows the splendid Terminal Building, in much the same way as Marina Bay Sands rises over the Fullerton Hotel, but size isn't everything. According to the URA, the Terminal Building was interpreted as a metaphor for a contemporary airplane. Opened in 1937, its cylindrical glass control tower, proudly elevated in the middle of the terminal, obviously resembled a cockpit. At the time, Old Kallang was not only Singapore's first civil airport, but also a key gateway between England and Australia and one of the finest airports in the world.

But it was a bit of a mess when I visited. To its credit, the URA gazetted the entire site, including the Terminal Building, the east and west blocks and the hangar in 2008, but the airport was lost amid the swanky developments around the Singapore Sports Hub and along the Kallang River to Tanjong Rhu. The People's Association had occupied the site until its move to Tyrwhitt Road in 2009 and the airport had been empty ever since. Kallang's development plans are constantly under review. The Singapore Biennale was held at the Terminal Building in 2011, which seemed a good fit; the iconic site is suited to hosting exhibitions and galleries. But its future is unlikely to be established until the Sports Hub has found its feet.

I made my way around the Terminal Building and considered climbing the perimeter fence, but there were signs and cameras everywhere. Singapore takes its state land protection extremely seriously. Whenever I see a vast, open grass field ripe for sports, picnicking and any number of outdoor activities and find the "state land, keep out" signs, I think of George Harrison's line to an overbearing park keeper in *A Hard Day's Night*.

"Sorry we hurt your field, Mister."

So I stepped back from Kallang Airport Way to fully take in the airport and wandered into the 1930s. I found a partially buried road. I checked my street directory. The road wasn't recorded. There was just a green square between Kallang Airport Way and Geylang Road. But it was clearly a road, with faded markings peering through the weeds and grasses that had spread across the kerb and spilled into the road's cracks. Litter and fallen branches covered the tarmac. In truth, the area was in a dreadful state. The trees that once lined the old road had snaked from one side to the other overhead, blocking out sunlight and adding to the gloominess. When I peered up, I noticed the original streetlamps. As I continued, I found stone gateposts with a lion's crest in the middle. And then the road abruptly stopped, filled in by a grassy slope. I found the location in my street directory again, but there was no reference. It was off the map, the road that cartographers forgot. I later discovered that this was the original road to the airport, leading Singapore's first cars from Geylang to the Terminal Building, passing through the stone gates and beneath the streetlamps. The URA has preserved the gates, the streetlamps and of course the major airport buildings. How the gazetted area will be redeveloped in the long-term remains to be seen, but there's no harm in going round the place with a lawnmower and a pair of secateurs in the meantime.

Still, the ghostly street from the 1930s is worth a quick visit. It's a scruffy oddball so close to a micro-managed city centre. Go see the lost road to the historic airport. And should you encounter any confused tourists, direct them towards Changi. The Old Kallang Airport is closed. No, really.

IF THE OLD KALLANG AIRPORT has been spared, those living near the Old Kallang Airport Road have not. The residents of 14 low-rise blocks in Dakota Crescent must be out by mid-2016. Dakota Crescent is a dying estate that no longer pays its way. But it's also one of Singapore's oldest, built in 1958 by the British and named after the Douglas DC-3 Dakota, a model of plane that once landed at the old airport across the road. When the Government announced its intention to demolish and redevelop the estate, Facebook pages and blog posts soon appeared. Never mind the neglect, think about the heritage, they cried. But the constituency MP made a telling point in reply.

Those who champion the heritage mostly do not live there.

But then nor do most of the policy-makers who decided to flatten the place.

Dakota Crescent suddenly represented Singapore's perennial struggle between conservation and commerce. Should cultural ties be tightened at every opportunity in the nation-building process? Or should we not, as my mum would say, save any old shit just for the sake of it?

Not that the Dakota Estate would ever be labelled as such, but it was certainly run down. As I made my way through its unsheltered garden, I picked out some of the retro aesthetics shared with Tiong Bahru, the folding doors, the angled balconies and the retro grilles. The architecture was unique and at least some of it was worth saving, but Dakota Crescent was not Tiong Bahru. On the plus side, the estate was spared the antique dealers and poodle pedicures.

But the neglect was inescapable. With many of the elder residents being beneficiaries, if that's the right word, of the Public Rental Scheme, the upgrading programmes had clearly not reached Dakota. The place was so archaic, I actually missed the lift twice. Thanks to its dark blue, windowless door and the absence of an electronic panel, I had assumed it was a store cupboard. It was only when the door unexpectedly opened and a Malay auntie stepped out pushing a shopping trolley that I jumped back in terror. It was one hell of a lift though. The chipboard wood panelling inside the narrow space was complimented by three protruding black buttons, indicating that it stopped only at floors one, three and six of the seven-floor blocks. And when the lift stopped, it informed me not with a slightly erotic, robotic voice, but by shuddering to a halt so violently, I let out a tiny scream.

I climbed the final flight of stairs to the top floor. The extraordinary view must have teased residents for years. The encroaching cityscape made the estate's demise inevitable. Once the city reached the Singapore Sports Hub, Dakota Crescent was just about done. The city had reached the doorsteps not of black and white bungalows or river-facing condos, but tired, ignored rental properties. Dakota Crescent never stood a chance.

Hopefully, the Dove can at least be spared. Quite unexpectedly, I had found the Dragon's twin. The father of Singapore's most iconic playgrounds, Khor Ean Ghee, had also spawned the Dove of Dakota Crescent to go along with Toa Payoh's Dragon. The square sandpit, the mosaic tiles around the head, the steel ribs for climbing and the arse-shredding concrete slide were all present and correct. If anything, the Dove playground was in slightly better condition, presumably because of the estate's older residents (though I'd pay good money to see a couple of aunties on the tyre swings). So the Dove must be saved. At best, the heritage playground might hope to share the Dragon's fate, left alone in a grassy field. As for the rest of the Dakota Crescent estate, well, it really depends on your point of view.

I joined an Indian uncle on a bench near the Dove playground. We savoured the peacefulness for a bit until I piped up.

"Uncle, how long you stay here?" I asked.

"More than 12 years," he whistled.

Most of his front teeth were missing. I'm not casting aspersions on his physical appearance. It's just that every time he spoke he sounded as if he were calling in a sheepdog.

"That's a long time."

"Yah," he whistled.

"But you must move out soon, right?"

"Yah."

He wasn't really a raconteur. He liked whistling though.

"You must be sad though, right," I continued, shamelessly steering him towards a heartfelt lament about the impending demolition of his historic home.

"Why?"

"It's Dakota Crescent. These flats were built in 1958."

"Too old, very troublesome, only got one lift, always breaking down."

"But these flats are iconic," I insisted, really labouring the point. "They are part of Singapore's history."

He gave me a wry, toothless grin.

"Ah, you youngsters want history. I want a lift that stops on each floor."

Of course he's right. I know he's right. He's a man in his 70s with a failing hip and an antiquated, mischievous lift. He's not interested in my First World problems. He has Third World memories. He's earned the right to retire in as much comfort as possible. But can we not make allowances for both sides? Dakota Crescent doesn't adequately serve its elderly population, but it could certainly open its funky folding wooden doors and hip '50s window frames to the nouvelle riche with more money than sense. Dakota Crescent could be a vibrant Tiong Bahru on the Geylang River, populated by hipsters and visited by Sports fans and concertgoers on weekends. Send in the cupcakes and the cappuccinos and the handcrafted batik made by a Javanese grandmother paid a fair wage in an eco-friendly village. Fill the communal gardens with potted plants, one-speed bicycles and free books and Dakota will immediately become a chic, bohemian community just 10 minutes from the city centre.

Tiong Bahru won't be able to touch it.

Dakota Crescent represents so much more than a historic housing estate. It's about iconic architecture. It's about our history being something more than photographs on the wall of a local library exhibition. Most of all, it's about a dove. We've gotta save the Dove.

For the benefit of tourists, this is the Old Kallang Airport. It is no longer open.

The Dakota Crescent blocks are original and make up one of the oldest housing estates in Singapore, but they will be gone soon.

If Dakota Crescent cannot be spared, can we at least save the Dove?

Twenty Three

HAVING SPENT the best part of six months on the road searching for the island's musty bits, I decided to buy my forgiving wife a present. So I headed for a popular side street that, until very recently, had never appealed. For years now, my wife has hailed Haji Lane. But I'd refused to accompany her on shopping expeditions for the usual childish reasons. I had assumed that the fashionistas had long annexed that particular corner of Kampong Glam. Poorer Muslims had been pushed out of their own background, the latte lovers had moved in and I naturally believed that the home furnishing boutiques all had a look and feel that suggested Laura Ashley had wandered past and thrown up over the window displays. My inverted snobbery held sway.

Haji Lane could keep its broccoli soup and shabby chic cushion covers.

But I was the main reason. I cannot be trusted in niche, hip, shopping outlets. The kid who grew up working in an East London café has a tendency to mutter unhelpful comments like: "You want $200 for a fucking table cloth?"

But the same kid also feels sorry for those same retailers sitting in empty stores. When I see them, I see the final days of my family's dying café. Pity consumes me. Suddenly, inexplicably, a

$200 round tablecloth is the very creature comfort that's been missing from my life. The fact that I do not own a round table is neither here nor there. About five years ago, a door-to-door saleswoman smooth-talked her way into my Australian living room and tried to sell me a vacuum cleaner. This vacuum cleaner cost $3,500. Our Australian car was worth less money. The single mother informed us that if she sold us the vacuum cleaner, she was eligible for a Gold Coast holiday with her son as a form of sales commission. The vacuum cleaner was undoubtedly impressive. The suction was truly terrifying, boasting the power to remove the hair from a man's chest. I leaned forward.

"Well, in that case," I began.

My wife squeezed my hand. She knew what was coming.

"Neil, can I have a word, please?"

We went into the kitchen.

"You are not buying it," she hissed.

"But the poor woman needs the commission," I implored. "She can take her boy to the Gold Coast."

"We've got a vacuum cleaner. And we only bought that one because you felt sorry for the salesman."

"But the poor woman…"

"It's $3,500."

"Have you seen the suction on that bad boy?"

"It's $3,500."

"And the chest-hair removal thing?"

"You buy it. I divorce you."

I didn't buy it. But I'll never forget the saleswoman's imploring eyes. I am a soft touch. Retailers sense my vulnerability. That's why my wife eventually dragged me to Haji Lane. She knew that I'd succumb in the quiet, indie shops and buy a sack-full of kitsch.

And I loved the place. Haji Lane was the little street that could.

The restored shophouses in a single, narrow lane behind Arab Street hit upon a subtle formula of discreetly combining old and new Singapore, the hip and the heritage, the obscenely rich and the cost-conscious. There might just be a model for other gentrified districts to follow. Of course, bars offer $25 cocktails and pretentious antique dealers will insist that a splintered, faded tea chest is not a splintered, faded tea chest but the side coffee table that's been missing from your dinner parties. But there are also the three-for-$10 clothes outlets that wouldn't look out of place in Toa Payoh Central. There's not only an eclectic mix at Haji Lane, there's a more egalitarian mix.

Besides, the revival of Kampong Glam around Haji Lane, Arab Street and Bussorah Street, also known as the Muslim Quarter, has been one of New Singapore's most uplifting successes. When I first arrived, the Singapore Tourism Board banged on about Chinatown and Little India, but the historic centres of the indigenous communities tended to command less attention (and visitors). To be frank, I always found the emphasis on Chinatown a little confusing in a country where almost 75 per cent of the people are, of course, Chinese. The Malays seemed to get the short end of the stick.

But Haji Lane was thriving when I visited. As it was early, the shops were just opening, but the tour parties from China had already arrived, in their luminous baseball caps and following their flag-waving tour guide. The temptation to raise an identical flag and lead the tour party off in a different direction never leaves me.

The shop names were just as entertaining. Haji Lane's shops are forever outdoing each other with eccentric names. I passed "Spoil Market" and "Wonderland Café", but my favourite remains the tattoo parlour called "Visual Orgasm". I once stood under the shop sign and asked my wife if she thought of me in the same way. I think she's still laughing.

I stopped outside a disturbing shop that sold military paraphernalia. There were posters of army fatigues and muscular, bronzed men brandishing various weapons, providing passers-by with the most homoerotic scenes since Sylvester Stallone and Dolph Lundgren stripped to the waist and applied the baby oil in *Rocky IV.* The store specialised in knives of various shapes and sizes, judging by the window displays. I peered through the door and noticed a greasy-haired guy perusing army hats and wondering perhaps if he'd ever talk to a woman.

But there's a place for homoerotic images of military men in Haji Lane, just as there's room for hair and nail salons, a smattering of high-end boutiques, bike shops and genuinely irreverent offerings. Outside one delightfully silly shop, I deliberated between buying a retro telephone resembling a stack of Charles Dickens hardbacks and a Volkswagen Kombi-shaped photo frame. That's the subtle advantage that Haji Lane has over other shopping stretches. Gentrification pecks away at its cafes and cocktail bars without robbing the place of its sense of humour. It sells funny stuff. Unlike some of the dreadfully earnest or exclusive places I've trudged through in self-proclaimed funky towns, the street doesn't take itself so seriously. Haji Lane proves that heritage and hip can co-exist. Its terrific architecture and indigenous history are tastefully preserved, but there's still space for photo frames shaped like a Volkswagen Kombi.

The resident tattooist said it best. Haji Lane is a bit of a visual orgasm.

Shops line both sides of Haji Lane. They sells picture frames shaped like a Volkswagen Kombi. No other reason is needed to go shopping there.

Street art is appreciated in the trendy Kampong Glam area, especially if it covers power cables.

Twenty Four

AS HE ADJUSTED my life jacket, the tanned, muscled middle-aged Chinese chap reminded me that there was always a slim chance that I could die. He had permission to take me onto the Kallang River. He didn't have permission for me to die.

"I'm always scolding the kids who forget to put on a life jacket," he said, shaking his head. "I tell them you can die, you know."

"Really?" I asked, gesturing towards the Kallang River. "The water looks calm."

He checked my life jacket again, eyeing the buckles and fasteners.

"Hey, it's no joke. One time some kayakers got trapped under a pontoon in Cambodia. Weren't wearing life jackets, couldn't get out. They drowned… Come, let's go kayaking."

I asked to go to the toilet first. The pep talk felt like a laxative. After relieving myself, I waited at the riverbank of the Kallang Water Centre. The placed buzzed with corporate dragon boaters in wraparound shades and eager kids and teenagers waiting for their kayak lessons. Across the Kallang Basin, rows of buoys marked out boating lanes, illuminated by the sun's reflection. Teachers barked instructions at kids in single kayaks as dragon boaters raced past them in the background. The smell of suntan lotion filled the air as tanned torsos and bulging biceps passed me, lifting oars and kayaks onto greasy shoulders. It was 9.30am on a Saturday morning. I had expected the Kallang River to be deserted. I had also never felt so white, scrawny and undernourished. Even the teenagers had glistening, vein-protruding forearms. I examined my pasty limbs and expected to find them entangled beneath a pontoon at some point.

"I'm Goh Eng Soon," said the tanned, muscled Chinese man. "I organise events and programmes for the Singapore Canoe Federation. How old do you think I am?"

"You'll never guess," said Lim Jun Ping, the chairman of the federation's coaching committee, joining us from his office.

This is always an impossible game to play. Obviously, the person presumes a certain youthfulness in physical appearance so the tendency is always to play safe and go low. But how low? The man was in good shape, but he didn't look 15.

"I'd say 40-plus," I offered. Always add the "plus", it ensures generous latitude.

"I'm 55," said Eng Soon proudly.

He was right. He did look exceedingly well for his age.

"I'm 40," I blurted out.

Eng Soon looked me up and down. "Yah, somewhere around there."

Jun Ping, who was several years younger than me and yet somehow balanced a full-time job at the Republic Polytechnic with his responsibilities as a chairman of the Singapore Canoe Federation, ushered me towards the scruffy boat yard. Canoes, kayaks and dragon boats were stacked in long, metallic racks.

"Which one do you want?" he asked.

"Erm… I'm not sure really."

Jun Ping looked across at me.

"You said you've got plenty of kayaking experience, right?"

"Well, when I go on holiday to Malaysia. I get one for an hour for 30 ringgit."

"And what sort of kayak do you hire?"

"A yellow one."

Jun Ping directed me towards a two-seater kayak and we carried it towards the pontoon. It was yellow.

As both men explained, no one can paddle on Singapore's rivers and selected reservoirs without permission, a permit or certification. I didn't have the last two so I had contacted the Singapore Canoe Federation for the first one. They kindly agreed to act as river guides and instructors, steering me away from buoys, dragon boats and pontoons.

In Australia, not surprisingly, a different, less nanny-like attitude prevails towards water sports and outdoor pursuits. Several years ago, I went into a sports store in Geelong and enquired about buying a kayak.

"So if I bought that yellow one there," I said to a teenaged sales assistant. "What would I have to do next?"

"Take it home."

"No, I mean, do I have to register it or anything?"

"Register it? It's a kayak, mate, not a Rottweiler."

"But when I lived in Singapore, you couldn't just buy a kayak and take it the nearest river. You needed a licence, permission. What do I do here?"

"Drop it onto the Barwon River, stick an oar in, put one arm in front of the other and try not to drown."

I never bought the kayak in the end. The kid kept laughing at me.

Eng Soon and Jun Ping never laughed at me. They just asked me not to touch anything. With the care usually devoted to a newborn being lowered into a lukewarm bath, they guided me onto the kayak. Together, Jun Ping and I pushed away from the pontoon. And for the first time in my life, I was paddling on one of Singapore's rivers.

I had always intended to finish the tour on water, rather than land. In a city-state where change is the norm and constancy is a dirty word, Singapore's rivers still flow. From the Orang Laut (sea gypsies) and the Bugis traders to Stamford Raffles and the dragon-boating bankers, life has revolved around the island's rivers. We've built beside them, over them and under them. We've traded on them, polluted them, neglected them, cleaned them, dammed them, widened them and even diverted them. Their importance was already being inscribed in an undecipherable language centuries ago on the Singapore Stone. In a country largely starved of natural resources, the rivers and subsequent reservoirs are one of the few assets that have retained their relevance, influence and importance.

In Old Singapore, it was the rivers' strategic location and the island's establishment as a free port. In New Singapore, it's about not bending over before the Malaysian water authorities and handing them the Vaseline. Collectively, the rivers remain the lifeline of a country and a literal link between Old and New Singapore. Land can be built on, reclaimed, reshaped, sold off, en-bloced and sold off again. Singapore's land will always ebb and flow. It's fluid and ever changing. But Singapore's rivers are solid as a rock, the same, consistent foundation for past, present and future. Just about everything on terra firma is fair game and up for sale. But, to paraphrase the Singapore Government when chatting with the neighbours, don't fuck with our water supply.

I set off with Jun Ping along the Kallang Basin towards the Kallang River, a once swampy area populated by the Orang Kallang, the sea nomads who lived on their fishing boats. Now the river was filled with corporate dragon boaters in branded singlets. That's economic progress for you.

But the trip was glorious. Under a cloudy sky, we paddled along with the breeze. We passed under the Merdeka Bridge and did that nodding and smiling thing that takes place between fellow outdoorsy enthusiasts. There was a real sense of camaraderie on the river, a mutual respect for a shared lifestyle. As Geylang Road approached overhead, we clambered aboard Eng Soon's rescue boat to explore the other rivers.

We powered through the Kallang Basin and into Marina Reservoir, passing the Gardens by the Bay before U-turning at the Marina Barrage and heading towards the Singapore River, with only a few kayakers and a couple of circling eagles for company. My hospitable companions shared stories of their ongoing struggles to cut red tape to get more Singaporeans onto the water. It was probably easier to get kids back in the water after they first saw *Jaws*. Never mind the difficulties involved in gaining permission from the relevant authorities to establish a kayaking coaching school for kids, just consider a fallen tree.

If a tree falls in a Singapore forest and no one is around to hear it, people shit themselves.

In a reservoir park, for instance, fallen trees are the responsibility of NParks. But whatever falls in the water is the responsibility of PUB. So one fallen tree requires two different departments to clear it away, possibly more. The Singapore Canoe Federation often deals with the PUB, NParks, the Singapore Land Authority, the URA, the Ministry of Education and even the Building & Construction Authority. If only the Orang Kallang fishing folks could see how complicated life was now on the Kallang River. Actually, they wouldn't be allowed to without a permit.

We left the Singapore River and ventured along the tranquil and surprisingly splendid Geylang River. We had the isolated stretch to ourselves. The narrow river made life difficult for turning dragon boats, so it was occasionally used by kayaking sprinters but otherwise left alone. Behind the protective barrier of overhanging tree branches, there was a splash, then another and a succession of ripples. Then we heard an unusual grinding, gnawing, tearing sound. Eng Soon turned off the engine and used an oar to steer the boat towards a leafy tree. Through the branches, we spotted an otter poking above the waterline. He paused for a moment to assess our size and distance. He judged us to be no threat and continued with his brunch.

With blood-soaked teeth, the otter ripped the head off a flapping fish and continued chewing.

Soon, we were surrounded. The sociable marine mammals had gathered for a mid-morning meal and swam, dived, fished and ate around the boat. I counted nine otters, endangered smooth otters no less, playing and eating together under the protection of an overhanging tree on the Geylang River. As Eng Hoon steered the silent boat, Jun Ping and I stretched out across its bow to marvel at the impudent creatures. We were three guys in a boat on a Singaporean river admiring the native wildlife. The serene scene was timeless. It was also accessible.

Like the otters, Old Singapore's gems are relatively easy to track down if you look in the right places. With some creative counting, I found 50 of my own. Some were obvious and straightforward to find, others were eccentric and remote. My improvised list of landmarks, locations, icons and idiosyncrasies say as much about my Singapore as it does about Old Singapore. That's as it should be. I spent a day on public transport to spend 15 minutes at a deserted bus stop in Choa Chu Kang.

I had my reasons. I'm weird.

And you'll have your own quirks and oddities that have had a profound impact on your life. They can't all be saved in any country, least of all a country with finite space and a warped obsession with population projections (I sometimes think decision-makers gleefully look at a map of Singapore in the way a chef might look at a turkey whilst clutching handfuls of sage and onion stuffing). But that doesn't mean we shouldn't at least try. I settled on 50 because someone mentioned the figure is of some importance in 2015, but there could be more. The recent opening of both the World War II tunnels in Woodlands and the Tanjong Pagar train station on public holidays are positive developments. Both would make my extended list of Old Singapore sites (as would the last kampong at Buangkok and Lim Chu Kang's Cashin House, wonderful locations I've previously explored).

You may disagree. Personal history and national history do not always overlap, a point often overlooked in some of the broad strokes applied to the SG50 celebrations. But do consider your choices. In the age of Buzzfeed, we love lists. Make your own. No two lists will be the same, but collectively, they all say the same thing. They are all in search of a soul.

That's been the greatest discovery on this heritage treasure hunt, finding Singaporeans who are seeking something beyond the rice bowl, reaching for something inexplicable, something intangible even, but something, anything, beyond the mundane. Perhaps it is the privilege and inevitable consequence of a First World nation no longer satisfied with a roof over the head and trains that mostly run on time. Perhaps a restless minority is afforded the pampered luxury of fretting over the biodiversity of an offshore reef or an obscure building's preservation, but that doesn't mean those activists should be mocked or dismissed for seeking an existence beyond pay cheques and 4D numbers.

Little by little, these Singapore heroes are trying to save what's left of their country, fighting for the big and small things that make Singaporeans Singaporean – from the Hantu Bloggers and the volunteer kayakers to the hundreds of Facebook pages, blogs and social media sites and petitions devoted to saving everything from Dakota Crescent and Beauty World Plaza to Lazarus Island and Toa Payoh's Dragon Playground (and The Dove at Dakota of course).

They're not quite ready to succumb to the shopping mall and its bland, stateless conformity. They're grateful for what they have, but it's not spiritually enriching. Thanks for the rice bowl and Farm Heroes, but what else have you got? More importantly, what else can we do to help? Can we save what already belongs to us? The National Heritage Board, NParks and the URA do commendable work in opening up World War II tunnels and saving colonial bungalows and shophouses, but the people's history, the heartlander's history, fares less well. Wealthy and well-meaning Peranakan benefactors preserve the spirit of Baba House, but the homes of Dakota Crescent and Siglap are less fortunate. (Both could be gone by the time you read this.) And the very birthplace of HDB – the first blocks completed by one of the most successful public housing programmes in the world – is in a dreadful state. Singapore's history feels like a battle won by an affluent, elitist minority.

As Singapore celebrates half a century, it cannot tell half a story. Modern Singapore didn't begin in 1965 or 1959, nor was it exclusively born at No. 38 Oxley Road (but Lee Kuan Yew's home must of course be preserved. If nothing else, I'd like to know what it feels like to walk on the other side of the road).

There is also a question to be asked of what kind of Singapore is being saved and for whom. The ceaseless advance of gentrification seems entirely at odds with a much trumpeted public housing policy that accommodates 80 per cent of the country. Yet the march of Jimmy Choo stilettos continues, stomping on long established business and rubbing them out like a discarded cigarette. Tiong Bahru always appears to be one more myopic rent increase away from being choked, suffering death by cappuccino. When the MRT arrives, Jalan Besar may endure a similar fate as the area gets ideas above its new station.

But the likes of Haji Lane, Baba House, Matilda House, Sungei Buloh, Lazarus Island, Upper Seletar Tower and even the rivers and reservoirs (with the right certification) are just about open and accessible to all. They all walk a tightrope, but at least there is one for others such as Joo Chiat, Coney Island and Old Changi Hospital to follow.

Compromise can of course be construed as weakness. Are nostalgia and sentimentality signs of economic vulnerability? Do they provide clear indications of a First World country going soft? Categorically, yes, and Singapore is all the better for it. The nation has followed the safety-first, economy-fixated approach for 50 years with unrivalled success, but has it made Singaporeans any happier? Those annual happiness indexes and snarling traffic jams might suggest otherwise. Perhaps there's an increasing desire to look past the dollars and cents towards something simpler, but more rewarding. Coney Island and Lazarus Island can be developed, but should they? Thieves Market could be closed for something more lucrative beside the new Jalan Besar station, but should it? Toa Payoh's Dragon Playground probably fails every modern health and safety check for a children's playground and the slides could leave kids needing skin grafts, but should it be knocked down? The island can bulldoze and demolish what's left of Old Singapore and replace the lot with condos, hotels and offices and foreigners will no doubt flock to one of the world's most popular tax havens. But when the umbilical cord between citizen and society is cut, when there are no longer any ties that bind, then there is nothing to keep Singaporeans here. In comparison, Johor's Iskandar region and Perth's far-flung suburbs suddenly look so inviting. Singaporeans may cash in and leave. If there's no cultural or spiritual investment, why should there be a financial one?

So these deserted housing estates, quirky shopping laneways and old-fashioned flea markets are more than just silly eccentricities. They keep us here. Without them, we return to the overriding questions that hang over Singapore's 50th anniversary. Who is all this for? Whether it's the rise of Marina Bay or the demise of Dakota Crescent, who is it for? Who profits? Is it the average man and woman on the street or a small, wealthy elite and their grateful foreign friends happy to indulge in Singapore's riches?

Many of the locations on my tour were crumbling, neglected and dishevelled. They were riddled with imperfections and almost certainly not cost-effective. But they remain, for the most part, uniquely Singaporean. They allowed me to write this unapologetically sentimental love letter to what's left of Old Singapore. I hope it doesn't become a time capsule.

Back on the boat, Jun Ping and I continued to lie on our bellies on the bow, watching the indefatigable otters dive in and out of the water. The Geylang River's breeze brushed across our backs. Aside from the otters splashing, the river was silent, a perfectly lazy Saturday afternoon. I turned towards Jun Ping.

"Just think. We could be in a shopping mall right now," I whispered.

But I was where I wanted to be. I had found a much sexier island. And it really is worth saving.

Old man of the river paddles through Old Singapore. As we sit on the Kallang River, I keep an eye on the camera. As you can see, Lim Jun Ping would rather keep his eye on me. (Photo by Goh Eng Soon.)

About the Author

Neil Humphreys grew up in Dagenham, England before travelling to Singapore when he was 21 for a short holiday. He stayed a bit longer and became one of the country's best-selling authors. His works on Singapore – *Notes from an Even Smaller Island* (2001), *Scribbles from the Same Island* (2003), and *Final Notes from a Great Island* (2006), the omnibus *Complete Notes from Singapore* (2007) and *Return to a Sexy Island: Notes from a New Singapore* (2012) – are among the country's most popular titles in the past decade. His book *Be My Baby* (2008) chronicled his journey to parenthood and was his first international best-seller. His three novels – *Match Fixer* (2010), *Premier Leech* (2011) and *Marina Bay Sins* (2014) – were also released to critical acclaim. When he's not peering through Singapore's nooks and crannies, he writes further adventures for his popular children's book series, *Abbie Rose & the Magic Suitcase*. He explains himself in further, excruciating detail here: www.neilhumphreys.net

Other Books by Neil Humphreys

NON-FICTION
Return to a Sexy Island
Singapore got sexy and the country's best-selling author got jealous. After five years chasing echidnas and platypuses in Australia, Neil Humphreys returns to Singapore to see if the rumours are true. Like an old girlfriend getting a lusty makeover, the island transformed while Humphreys was away. He goes in search of new Singapore, visiting locations that either did not exist five years ago or had been extensively rebuilt, renovated or revamped in his absence. Written with Humphreys' characteristic honesty and wit, this book is an insightful account of new Singapore.

Notes from an Even Smaller Island
Knowing nothing of Singapore, a young Englishman arrives in the land of "air-conned" shopping centres and Lee Kuan Yew. He explores all aspects of Singaporean life, taking in the sights, dissecting the culture and illuminating each place and person with his perceptive and witty observations.

Scribbles from the Same Island
Humphreys is back with yet more observations and ruminations about the oddball aspects of Singapore and its people. *Scribbles* also contains a selection of his work as a humour columnist.

Final Notes from a Great Island
All good things must come to an end, and before Humphreys makes his move Down Under, he revisits all the people and places he loves in his final, comprehensive tour of Singapore.

Complete Notes from Singapore (The Omnibus Edition)
All three of Humphreys' bestselling works, *Notes from an even Smaller Island*, *Scribbles from the Same Island* and *Final Notes from a Great Island*, in one classic, updated book.

Be My Baby: On the Road to Fatherhood
Follow Humphreys on his most terrifying and hilarious journey yet—travelling the unfamiliar road to fatherhood.

FICTION
Marina Bay Sins
Detective Inspector Stanley Low investigates a sadistic sex murder-suicide at Singapore's most prestigious hotel that plunges him back into a sordid underworld he was desperate to leave behind. He has no choice. Dead bodies at Marina Bay Sands are bad for business. They ask questions of a sanitised society no one is keen to answer. An intelligent, thought-provoking novel, this is Humphreys at his satirical best.

Match Fixer
Once a promising graduate of the West Ham United Academy and tipped to play for England, Chris Osbourne arrives on the Singapore football scene in a bid to right his faltering football career. But nothing has prepared him for the underground party drugs scene, the bent bookies, dubious teammates and a seductively beautiful journalist who welcome him to life in paradise.

Premier Leech
English Football Clubs are dying but club captain, Scott, couldn't give a toss. As long as he delivers on the pitch, he can do whatever he likes off it. That's the right and privilege of an English Premier League footballer—until he sleeps with his best mate's wife. The

tabloids go wild and a team of reporters are hot on the trails of both Scott and his manager, Charlie, who's been lining up a secret takeover with a Saudi businessman more interested in property and prostitutes than football. In a world where the only currency is fame, how much are they willing to sacrifice to stay in the game?

ABBIE ROSE & THE MAGIC SUITCASE

In this children's book series Abbie Rose travels to faraway places and goes on many adventures with her best friend Billy through the help of a magic suitcase.

The Day A Panda Really Saved My Life

Four-year Abbie Rose takes off on a journey of discovery with her magic suitcase. Join her as she learns all about the panda and travels magically to the mountains where pandas live. Abbie Rose and her best friend Billy come face to face with a panda, who comes to the rescue to save his new friend.

I Trapped A Dolphin But It Really Wasn't My Fault

Abbie Rose goes to the ocean with her best friend Billy. In the ocean, they see many different types of fishes and even meet a dolphin. Abbie Rose accidentally traps Billy and the dolphin in a fishing net but she manages to free it with the help of another new friend. Finally the dolphin is reunited with his family.

Picking Up A Penguin's Egg Really Got Me Into Trouble

Abbie Rose goes on an exciting adventure to the South Pole with her best friend Billy. There she meets a family of penguins. She picks up a penguin egg and the adventure begins. Abbie Rose and some penguins get separated from the rest of the group and come across a leopard seal that tries to eat them. In the end, Billy saves everyone and the penguins are reunited with their family.